ENTER
OURSELVES
TO DEATH?

The crisis in Christian Youth Culture

ANDREW STROM

RevivalSchool

ENTERTAINING OURSELVES TO DEATH?

First published online, 1998
First printing, 2008

Published by: Revival School
www.revivalschool.com

Wholesale distribution by Lightning Source, Inc.

ISBN-13: 978-0-9799073-4-0

ISBN-10: 0-9799073-4-9

1. Christian Life: Pop Culture Issues

2. Christian Ministry: Youth

CONTENTS:

Chapter One

BLIND TO COMPROMISE

I remember one time in the early 1990s, as I was shooting a music video for a local Christian band, standing on the stage and video-taping all the kids stage-diving and slam-dancing to the music. At the time I thought it was great - Christianity finally becoming 'relevant' to the youth culture of our day. And this was not an isolated case. In fact, I was aware through my activities in Christian band management and concert promotion at the time that there was a huge Christian youth culture out there that was very much devoted to "partying", raging and alternative fashion almost as an entire Christian lifestyle. After all, isn't such "relevance" the only real way we are going to reach the young people of today?

Since then, this whole "Christian partying" spirit has become bigger by the year. And it has spawned a whole generation of Christian bands who are quite happy to cater to the partying whims of their youthful fans. In fact, it could be said that an entire generation of Christians (35 years of age and under) are now growing up believing this to be a "normal" and healthy Christian way of life.

Both my wife and I have been musicians for many years, and we began our own Christian alternative band at about that same time (the early 1990s) with the express purpose of getting into the secular clubs and playing our music there. But in order to accomplish this, we knew we had to 'tone down' our lyrics and cover up the overt Biblical references, etc. I had no problem with doing this at the time. After all, we knew many other bands who had done the same. And so, another in the long line of modern Christian bands who never (or almost never) talk about Jesus was born. And yes, we did succeed in playing the secular clubs that I had so wanted to play. The question, "Where is God in all of this?" almost never crossed my mind at the time.

It took many months for God to get me to slow down enough to listen to what He was trying to say to me. (In fact, it took a series of disasters). But when He finally got my full attention, it didn't take Him long to start pin-pointing the deep motives behind what I was doing. The major thing that became obvious almost straight away was that at the very heart of our band lay one massive, deadly principle: COMPROMISE! This really was at the core of everything we were doing.

As you can imagine, when God showed me this with such clarity I was utterly devastated. I had been a committed Christian for many years, studying Revival and believing that something must be done to reach the youth. But here I was, compromising in order to get our music across. And I knew that much of the modern church's youth ministry was heading down the same road, in various ways.

We did eventually get back into playing music with a band, but things are now very different in many ways.

This book has been written to address several questions that I believe to be paramount in regard to current youth ministry and the Christian music industry. In fact, I believe that overall the Western church is heading down a path that is so ill-conceived and so fraught with danger that it has the potential to undermine everything that historic Christianity stands for. The youth of today are the leaders of tomorrow. Just exactly what kind of Christianity are they learning to practice in today's environment? And what have we achieved if we succeed in making our Christianity "cool", but raise a generation who know nothing of deeply seeking God? Is there a place for 'taking up the cross' and 'death to self' alongside worldliness, hedonism and carnality? Is God the great 'fun' party-man, or is He expecting a little more from us than simply hedonistic shallowness? Just exactly what is becoming of the young today, and what does God expect us to do about it? All these questions and more will be examined in the following pages.

Chapter Two

ENTERTAIN, ENTERTAIN, ENTERTAIN

Before I get any further into this controversial subject, I just want to say a little bit more about myself and my own background. As you may have picked up in the previous chapter, I have a long history of involvement with Christian bands, song-writing, recording, video and Youth-ministry, etc. Although I believe in a thoroughly biblical worldview and lifestyle, I would definitely be considered a modern Christian who lives in the modern world. In fact, I am convinced that radical measures are needed to bring today's church into the kind of state that will truly impact our culture and bring glory to God. I not only believe in the desperate need for true repentance and Revival in the church, but also of a thorough 'Reformation', so that today's church might become the kind of threat to the devil that she was always meant to be.

As a modern Christian musician, I do believe that the original message of the gospel must be made "relevant" to each new generation. But I also have to say that I have become deeply concerned in recent times, that much of what we call "relevance" in the church today, is really little more than 'hip' worldliness, compromise, and a desperate attempt to impress the world on its own shallow, hedonistic terms, rather than anything godly. In 1993, the well-known evangelical preacher John MacArthur put out a book entitled 'Ashamed of the Gospel' (subtitled, "When the church becomes like the world"). Obviously, because it was written by a known Conservative, many modern leaders may have found it easy to bypass this book's insights and warnings. But when I read it I found it an incisive and devastating exposé of much that is now occurring in Christendom. In it, MacArthur writes: "Traditional methodology - most noticeably preaching - is being discarded or downplayed in favor of newer means, such as drama, dance, comedy, variety, side-show histrionics, pop-psychology, and other entertainment forms... In the past half-decade, some of America's largest evangelical churches have employed worldly gimmicks like slapstick, vaudeville, wrestling exhibitions and even mock striptease to spice up their Sunday meetings. No brand of horseplay, it seems, is too outrageous to be brought into the sanctuary. Burlesque is fast becoming the liturgy of the pragmatic church."

Many Christians reading this may well be asking, "What is wrong with that? What is wrong with entertaining people in order to woo them into the kingdom?" These are seemingly valid questions, but I would like to raise some others that I believe to be even more pertinent: What effect does it have on our gospel, our overall message, and the lifestyles of Christians, when we begin to center our meetings on entertainment, rather than on sharp-edged spiritual truth? (Obviously, it is the youth who are most affected by this today). And what effect does it have when we begin to use marketing techniques and musical hype rather than historic gospel truths to "sell" Jesus? Is it just harmless fun, or is it part of a trend that is undermining just about every gospel truth that Christians have fought and died for over the centuries? (Please remember, I am writing this as one who has been involved in all this from the inside).

In many churches today, it is seemingly no longer 'positive' enough (in the modern TV-marketing sense of the word) to emphasize the cross, deep repentance, holiness, "death to self" and all the other meaty elements of basic Christianity which the New Testament emphasizes again and again. And so we change everything (even the very essence of the gospel itself) to fit the spirit of the age in which we live. "People don't want to hear about all that negative 'sin' stuff anymore," we reason. "We'd better preach things that win them over in a positive, modern way." Thus, the epidemic of preachers who seem to sound more and more like television commercials every week: "Come to Jesus, He will make you happy, He will fulfill the desires of your heart, He will comfort you, He will satisfy you, etc, etc." There is almost no difference here to the sentiments expressed in your average toothpaste commercial, but the most alarming thing of all is that many preachers seemingly wouldn't care even if there was. They cannot see what an enormous effect this 'marketing' approach is having on the very nature and content of the gospel they preach, and thus on the lives of the Christians all around them. Their attitude often seems to be: 'Whatever brings them in the door is OK by me.' This is the very attitude that has led to what I believe is a crisis of colossal proportions amongst today's Christian youth.

As I have said, today much of this error is flooding into the church under the guise of "relevance". In the name of 'relevance' we are rushing around desperately trying to make our music "cool" and our leadership style "cool" and our gospel "cool" and our youth events "cool", etc, etc - all in an effort to attract the world on it's own terms. None of this is of God at all. It relies almost entirely on the 'arm of the flesh'. It is really nothing less than worldliness and compromise in a new and very subtle (yet deadly) form.

Instead of "holier than thou", it seems like we are now expected to be "cooler than thou". Our whole effort is aimed at proving to the world that Christianity is just as cool, just as much shallow fun, just as much of a party, as the world has to offer. And so, to prove all this, we have to entertain and entertain and entertain. We feel we have to become just like the world, in order to impress the world on its own terms. Thus, we now need to be seen in fashionable (or better-still, 'hip' or alternative) clothes. And our youth events become an excuse for a "party". And our presentations become entertaining multi-media extravaganzas. All in an effort to equal or "out-cool" the world. (Which is why you now see 'moshing' heads, slam-dancing and stage-diving at our youth concerts - matching the world on it's own mindless, hedonistic terms. "Lovers of pleasures more than lovers of God"). Like I said, cool pride, worldliness and rebellion - all in the name of "relevance". JUST LIKE THE WORLD IN EVERY SENSE. Does this sound like God to you?

Of course, many of those promoting (often unwittingly) this "cool" approach have only the best intentions in doing so. They see that Christianity is no longer the force in society that it is meant to be, and that the church is largely mocked and ridiculed as being of little account or value in today's world. So they subconsciously try to address this by making their Christianity "cool" in worldly terms. Unfortunately, many of these 'cool' Christians do not realize that in order to impress the world on these terms, they have to compromise some of the most vital elements of New Testament Christianity. Like me, they often do not realize this until it is too late. And by then, the world's values have flooded in through the doors. The fact is, it is the things that are DIFFERENT about Christianity that make it so attractive (if the church is doing its job properly), not the things that are the same as the world. But from what we see occurring in the church at present, we have to conclude that more and more, the spirit of this age is utterly dominating the message of the church. And this simply cannot be allowed to continue.

As history clearly shows, if the devil cannot bind or deceive the church by pushing her to extremes in one direction, then he will gladly push her as far as he can the opposite way. If he cannot bind her with legalism and spiritual pride (i.e., the leaven of the Pharisees), then perhaps he will have more success in pushing her to the extremes of spiritual "license", the casting off of restraint, etc. It is my belief that this is exactly what has occurred in much of the Western church over the past fifteen years or so (particularly in evangelical, Charismatic and 'Third Wave' circles). The 1970's was a period of very heavy, authoritarian leadership and legalism in many churches (with the 'covering - submission' teaching, etc). But in the 1980's and 1990's, the dangers of legalism, heavy pastoral domination, and spiritual pride have been so thoroughly exposed in much of this branch of Christendom (particularly in the youth area) that there has arisen the opposite danger. (Which is just as deadly, as history clearly demonstrates).

It is my belief that in recent years, many of our Christian youth leaders have essentially reacted against the old 'straight-laced' style of Christian leadership, and have instead gone right over to the other extreme (i.e., they have become over-accommodating and completely anti-authoritarian, wanting to be seen as modern, open-minded, 'hip', and dynamic. Thus "authority" has become a dirty word). As always, this has created a huge vacuum of real authority, which the devil has been quick to exploit. As I said before, the fruits of this modern "cool" Christianity are: Worldliness, rebellion, compromise, soulishness, carnality, etc.

The Scripture, "they sat down to eat and drink, and rose up to play" has, in recent years, become very applicable to large sections of the modern church. Many of our young people in particular have never known anything else but a kind of shallow, "good times" Christianity. They can often be found 'raging it up large' at modern youth events and concerts, not because they are just so passionate in their deep worship of God, but rather because they really enjoy riding the shallow "buzz" of the music, etc. It is very clear that this whole "cool" thing comes from the 'spirit of this world', not from God.

And it is not just the youth who have succumbed to this shallow "partying" spirit. It is apparent that many of the older ones have now also given themselves over to it. Anyone who objects to this "party-time" emphasis in the church is soon labeled sneeringly as being 'legalistic' or judgmental. Like the youth of the sixties, we are now being told to just 'let go' (if it feels good, do it), etc. We are told that in doing so, we are breaking free from tradition and religion. But I am convinced that all we have essentially done is exchanged one set of spiritual chains for another. (Remember that I write this as a fairly 'liberated' modern musician myself. I am not at all "anti" most Rock music or youth culture, but I am certainly against the kind of shallow 'casting off of restraint' that we are seeing in today's churches. This can only ever lead to deep spiritual deception).

It was Pentecostal pioneer Frank Bartleman who lamented, concerning the early Pentecostal movement: "As the movement began to apostatize platforms were built higher, coat tails were worn longer, choirs were organized, and string bands came into existence to 'jazz' the people. The kings came back once more, to their thrones, restored to sovereignty. We were no longer 'brethren'. Then the divisions multiplied..." And as Samuel Chadwick has so insightfully stated: "A religion of mere emotion and sensationalism is the most terrible of all curses that can come upon any people." It had actually been prophesied in the 1906 'Azusa Street' Revival that: "In the last days three things will happen in the great Pentecostal Movement: 1) There will be an over-emphasis on power, rather than on righteousness; 2) there will be an overemphasis on praise, to a God they no longer pray to; 3) there will be an overemphasis on the gifts of the Spirit - rather than on the Lordship of Christ." Clearly, the truth of this is now tragically evident for all to see. And it is the youth who are largely bearing the brunt of the church's Laodicean decline (though they hardly know it).

For those who have wondered why many popular Christian musicians these days seemingly want to be seen as 'cool' more than they want to talk about seeking God (with some exceptions), I hope that the above paragraphs will give you some insight as to why this might be. The church is losing the battle for the hearts and minds of today's youth. And even those whom we do have are often not encouraged or taught to be true DISCIPLES of Christ, but rather mere adherents (often in name only). The devil is ripping the rug out from under us, and the spirit of the age is dominating the church, so that we feel we have to conform to the world's pattern by becoming an "entertainment center" (just like any secular group or club) in order to attract members. Is this what the early church did? And is this truly what Jesus would want?

Chapter Three

A CHRISTIAN YOUTH CRISIS

It is my firm conviction that the massive changes that have come over modern youth ministry in the last twenty years or so, have already begun to bear a bitter harvest, and will continue to do so for many years to come unless drastic steps are taken. In fact, things have now become so bad in my view, that what we are facing could well be termed a Christian youth 'crisis' of huge proportions. Why would I term it a crisis? Isn't it true that we are still attracting good numbers to our youth events and concerts, etc? Yes, there is little problem with QUANTITY. If it is a 'numbers' game, we are not doing too bad. But what kind of success is it, if all we largely do is gather and entertain large groups of young people with very few of them ever becoming true DISCIPLES of Jesus Christ? Jesus said: "Go into all the world and make DISCIPLES of all nations..." Surely this has to be the test of how effective a ministry really is. And using this criteria, any ministry that is not producing genuine DISCIPLES of Jesus has to be viewed as an abject failure, surely?

Speaking of the huge Christian Greenbelt Festival held regularly in England, musician John Allen stated: "It seems undeniable that most of the audience is there simply to enjoy the music, not to think hard about anything; and there is a real danger of the emergence of the 'Greenbelt Christian', the semi-converted, shallowly committed teenager whose Christianity means little more than that he enjoys festival-going." What a tremendously significant statement! And the tragic fact is, that such 'Greenbelt Christians' are now found in their multiplied thousands right around the globe. For it is not just the large festivals that have succumbed to this spirit of entertainment. We now find this 'entertain-them-at-all-costs' approach to youth ministry everywhere, from local church youth groups right up to large regional gatherings. This spirit has pervaded everything, particularly those areas in the church that are connected with young people. In fact, it has become increasingly rare to find gatherings of Christian youth now in which these attitudes do not prevail.

But the staggering thing about this is that all we are doing is imitating a world that many young people are growing increasingly wary of. We live in a society today in which teenagers are almost entertained to death, from the time they wake up to the time they go to bed. And many young people are growing increasingly jaded and cynical because of it. Every year, the movies and television strive to outdo themselves with more and greater spectacular effects and explosions, and every year the makers of video games come up with graphics that are even more realistic than the year before. Every year, the children are being hyped to buy and consume at a greater rate - toys and games that are brighter, funnier, faster, more spectacular. And all we are doing by trying to conform our Christianity to this approach, is playing on the world's turf by it's own mind-numbing rules. And ultimately, we will always lose. I am convinced that what young people will respond to today is not a Christianity that involves more worldliness, more entertainment, more hoopla, and a greater desperation to be "cooler than thou". They can get plenty of this elsewhere. What is attractive about true Christianity is the things that are DIFFERENT - the things like true cleansing, eternal forgiveness, an intimate relationship with God, and battling on behalf of righteousness and truth, which CANNOT BE FOUND ANYWHERE ELSE. These are the things that will make true DISCIPLES out of today's young people. But do we dare preach it this way?

What we are actually doing by trying to make our Christianity more worldly, is placing it at a great disadvantage. We are stripping it of the things that historically have made the Christian faith so appealing and powerful. I am also convinced that more than anything else, today's jaded youth will respond to a CHALLENGE. In fact, I am convinced that the greater the challenge, the more interest and the greater level of discipleship there will be. What today's "amused-to-death" young people need desperately is a cause worth fighting and even dying for - a cause that calls them to deny themselves and to live a life of radical obedience to God. Jesus Christ is that cause. And if we don't provide such a challenge to today's jaded generation, then don't be surprised if some much darker cause arises to steal their allegiance. In many ways, today's youth, raised for much of their lives in a spiritual and moral vacuum, are truly ripe for the picking. And the devil knows this very well. If we are not willing to provide the youth with a cause worth fighting for, then he surely will.

The results of worldly or "cool" Christianity amongst our youth are now clearly visible for all to see. You only have to visit just about any large gathering of Christian young people in the Western world today to see that many of them do not take their Christianity terribly seriously at all. They are often there for the 'buzz', for what they can get out of it, and they have been conditioned not to want anyone much "preaching" to them. Most of them seem far more interested in surfing, clothes, partying, skateboards, cars, music, snowboards or fashion than they do in the foundational teachings of Jesus. What we are actually doing is "immunizing" many of these young people against the true gospel and against full discipleship. (Of course, many who have been brought up in the church have imbibed the "cool Christianity" ethos, and are now deliberately doing all they can to make Christianity 'cool' in the eyes of the world).

There has always been a 'social' aspect to the Western church that has attracted a certain 'club' membership. But this is different. This is an epidemic, and it is being encouraged right from the very top down. Many pastors and youth leaders have concluded that it is best to give the young people what they seem to want, just so they can get the numbers in the door. And the problem is growing worse, not better. Unless something drastic is done, all I can personally see on the horizon is years and years of such continual shallowness that we end up with churches full of people who desire little else but 'ear-tickling', entertaining preaching and crowd-pleasing (rather than God-pleasing) "worship". In actual fact, this is already a reality on such a massive scale in today's Western church, that it begs the question of whether true, historic Christianity can even survive much longer without being utterly swamped by the prevailing hedonism and selfishness. Despite what we are being told, things really are that serious. True, historic Christianity is in terrible danger on many fronts. Unless something dramatic occurs, I see only years of increasing lukewarmness, shallowness and compromise ahead.

What does it mean to be a true disciple of Jesus? The gospels are very clear on this point. Jesus stated on a number of occasions that in order to be his disciple, we must "deny ourselves, take up our cross and follow Him." The standard of heart commitment, faith and courage required is HIGH, not low. In fact Jesus clearly stated, "Unless you give up all that you have you cannot be my disciple" (Lk 14:33). This was certainly not a "lowest common denominator" message at all. But you would never know it, from the standards that prevail in many of today's Christian youth gatherings. When was the last time you attended a modern youth event and heard a message on deeply seeking God, denying self, taking up the cross, genuine holiness, etc? (Actually, despite being an essential part of basic New Testament Christianity, many of these topics are almost sneered at amongst the advocates of "cool Christianity". Not worldly or 'entertaining' enough, I guess).

I have to be frank and say that when I look at the overall situation in today's church, I am reminded very much of the Scriptures warning of apostasy and lukewarmness in the last days: "For the time will come when they will not endure sound doctrine; but after their OWN LUSTS shall they heap to themselves TEACHERS, HAVING ITCHING EARS" (2 Tim 4:3). Jesus warned the last church, the Laodicean church in Revelation that, "because you are lukewarm, and neither cold nor hot, I WILL SPEW YOU OUT OF MY MOUTH. Because you say, I am rich and increased with goods, and have need of nothing" (Rev 3:16-17). And speaking of the day of Judgment, Jesus said: "Many will say to me in that day, Lord, Lord, have we not prophesied in your name, and in your name cast out many demons, and in your name done many wonderful works? And then will I say to them, I never knew you. DEPART FROM ME, YOU EVIL-DOERS" (Mt 7:20-21).

Surely the lament of Jesus found in Mt 15:8 is just as applicable today as it was then: "This people draw nigh to me with their mouth and honor me with their lips, but their heart is far from me." Where are those amongst today's youth ministries who will stand up and be counted for the Lord and His truth in our day?

Chapter Four

THE CHRISTIAN MUSIC SCENE

Over the last three decades, Christian contemporary music has grown to become a colossal INDUSTRY, with it's own record companies, "star" artists, radio stations, rock festivals, autograph signings, hype, glossy magazines, merchandising, etc, etc. Obviously, much of this is potentially harmful to true spirituality while some of it is not. As Tom Morton (then a full-time musician with British Youth for Christ) wrote: "What has happened over the last fifteen years in Britain has been the formation of a Christian music 'scene'... Instead of this subculture being rooted in Christian standards in fact as well as in name, it appears that some of the Christian music scene has become, in effect, sub-Christian. Some Christian musicians seem excessively concerned with fame, with their image; some record companies seem profit-oriented at the expense of their artists' ministries, and since their 'package' is wrapped up in pseudo-evangelical language and justification, few people have realized what was happening." He also wrote that: "The rock music industry is perhaps one of the most corrupt in existence, and the unthinking transfer of its techniques to the Christian sphere has resulted in some of the uneasy mixtures of gospel and garbage which have in the past gone under the name of 'gospel concerts.'"

Many Christians may not realize that in America, every one of the major Christian music companies is now owned by a secular corporation. EMI owns Sparrow, Starsong, Forefront and Gospocentric, Gaylord Entertainment owns Word Records, and the Zomba Group owns Benson Music, Brentwood Music and the Reunion label. This may not be as severe a problem as it may first appear, but it certainly raises questions as to whether these Christian labels are now essentially profit-driven or ministry-driven entities. And it also gives a pointer to just how much MONEY is involved in the Christian music industry today.

Certainly, there is now real money to be made by artists in the Christian music scene. And this must surely be a source of temptation to many, perhaps turning their attention more and more onto material concerns rather than spiritual ones. For instance, in the old days it may have been purely for the love of God that a musician would go on tour with their music and their message. But now they know that a tour can make thousands of dollars and help them sell thousands of records. Couldn't this have a debilitating effect on the spirituality and motivation of the artists concerned?

It is well-known throughout Christendom that tragically, the lives of many "superstar" preachers, musicians and Christian celebrities are often not what they appear to be. Sadly, a number have succumbed to the temptations of money, women, or pride, and their lives are a hollow travesty of what they present to the public. There is ample testimony to the fact that many Christian recording artists are not immune to these dangers either, and life on the road can present many pitfalls to those who are not absolutely anchored upon the Rock of Christ. In fact, singers and musicians can be exposed even more to these temptations, in that they can become "idolized" by their Christian fans in a manner that is frankly sickening to behold (particularly coming from believers), and certainly very unhealthy for the artists concerned.

The well-known prophetic musician Keith Green wrote: "The only music ministers to whom the Lord will say, 'Well done, good and faithful servant' are the ones whose lives prove what their lyrics are saying, and the ones to whom music is the least important part of their life - glorifying the only worthy One has to be the most important." He also wrote: "Who lives more comfortably and has more 'fans' than the latest bright and shining gospel star?... Quit trying to make gods out of music ministers, and quit trying to become like those gods. The Lord commands you to 'Deny yourself, take up your cross daily, and follow me.'" We all know how much God hates idolatry. Yet so many of today's Christian music "stars" are treated in ways that are tantamount to 'hero-worship'. I ask you, will God deal lightly with such blatant idolatry and sin? I think not.

The following hard-hitting report by Stacy Saveall on the annual 'Creation' Christian music festival was sent to me a number of years ago - but is still very relevant today:

"My family and I just returned from our annual vacation trip to the rural mountains of Pennsylvania here in the U.S., where the largest Christian music festival in the world is held each year. About 50-60 thousand people gathered to camp out and listen to speakers and music...

While we have attended the festival for the past several years, last year and this year in particular my spirit was greatly troubled by what I observed... the most disturbing aspect of this whole event was the rampant commercialism and outright idolatry tied to the Christian music.

As I walked thru the huge crowds during the concerts and watched, I saw hawkers making their way among the young, selling eight-inch glow-in-the-dark green crosses. Young teens would line up for a half-mile to get the autographs of the Christian stars. A sign posted near the front of the line read "No Hugging" and "No Pictures".

Ironically, one night as Michael W. Smith sang and then spoke from the stage about his moving experiences in a poor South African children's hospital, hundreds of teenage girls could be heard screaming in ecstasy from the rear of the concert field as the group Jars of Clay arrived for their autograph signing session. It was a truly watershed moment. It was as if the Lord was showing those present there was a choice to be made here.

Later, several hundred teens "moshed" and slammed into each other during a Supertones "ska" concert as less than 100 attended a concurrent praise and worship session.

To be sure, many of these groups make an effort to say it is not they who are to be worshipped. Some then however, head off to the autograph booth. Their t-shirts, CDs and posters are on display for sale in huge quantities. I was even accosted by a young entrepreneur, about 12 years old, selling "Redemption" cards, a Christian alternative to the "Magic" cards that have swept the secular marketplace.

If Christ were present I'm sure he would have been turning over the tables...

In closing, I must say an honest effort of evangelism remains at the event. Greg Laurie spoke on the closing night and hundreds accepted the invitation. Over a thousand children were sponsored at the Compassion International booth. There were some young groups that eschewed the star treatment and strove for true musical worship (Caedmon's Call for one), but we need to show increasing discernment in these matters."

On Reformation Day, 31 October 1997, well-know American Christian singer Steve Camp released his controversial "Call for Reformation for the Contemporary Christian Music Industry", which he inserted as a poster in the American CCM Update magazine shortly after. In this 'Call for Reformation' Camp argues that contemporary Christian music has abandoned its original calling from the Lord and left the biblical standard for ministry. He states his belief that "the serpentine foe of compromise has invaded the camp through years of specious living, skewed doctrine and most recently secular ownership of Christian music ministries."

Although he acknowledges that there are godly men and women who love the Lord that work and record for the Christian music companies, Camp also states that the Christian music industry "finds itself on a slippery slope sliding away at accelerated speeds from the Savior." He says that in the early days contemporary Christian music's lyrics unashamedly declared Jesus Christ as Lord, but that now a "biblical illiteracy" rules the day. He also asserts that "departure from the Word of God is now clearly evidenced in our music, lyrics, business practices and alliances." He calls the industry to repent of its sins or face God's judgment. "Let us come together to make history to make contemporary Christian music ... Christian again".

Camp also makes some unrestrained and even outrageously controversial statements at times: *"Christian music, originally called Jesus Music, once fearlessly sang clearly about the gospel. Now it yodels of a Christless, watered-down, pabulum-based, positive alternative, aura-fluff, cream of wheat, mush-kind-of-syrupy, God-as-my-girlfriend kind of thing... The CCMI [contemporary Christian music industry] has committed spiritual adultery in joining itself with the wayward world in trying to forward the message of the gospel. This has and will prove to be fatal for Gospel music, as we know it today... We cannot partner with the unbelieving world in a common spiritual enterprise or ministry. To harness unbelievers and believers in a Christ-centered endeavor is to be unequally yoked... Undiscerning believers think it is a profound ministry strategy to join forces with unregenerate people in forwarding the gospel. Unwittingly, they harness Jesus Christ, the Worthy One, with Belial or Satan, the worthless one, in an unholy alliance, the very essence of being unequally yoked."*

We will speak more about the pitfalls and also the possibilities of this intermarriage between the secular and the Christian record companies later in this book. Coincidentally, just two weeks after Camp's bold 'Call for Reformation', it was announced by the organizers of the 21-year-old Jesus Northwest festival (which attracted up to 30,000 people each year) that they were closing down the festival for spiritual reasons. In a press release announcing their decision, the Executive Director of Jesus Northwest, Randy Campbell said:

"For the past three years we have had a growing unrest with the focus of ministry at Jesus Northwest. In the fall of 1996 the Lord began to call our church to a deeper walk of faith and holiness. As

He continued to reveal more of His presence and character to us, much of the ministry and direction of our church began to change.

Because Jesus Northwest is such a large ministry of Peoples Church, it was obviously affected by these changes. Initially we questioned Jesus Northwest's validity because of our growing concern over the worldliness and idolatry we had watched, allowed and even facilitated. We knew the Lord was stirring something in us regarding Jesus Northwest, but for many months we did not clearly understand what it was. As the festival drew closer, we began to see glimpses of the fact that the problems with Jesus Northwest were not simply within the festival environment itself, but many had to do with us as a body...

Our concern over the idolatry we saw at the festival, such as believers exalting artists and speakers, was now over-shadowed by the reality that Jesus Northwest had become an idol to our church. The festival had come between us and the direction and heart of the Lord.

On Sunday, July 27, 1997, the Lord directed our Senior Pastor to lead our church body into a time of corporate and public repentance for what we had done. We sensed the Lord calling us to lay the ministry of Jesus Northwest at His feet and to begin to truly trust Him for His will and purpose. We are continuing in that process, but sense at this time He would also have us repent to those in the body of Christ we have endeavored to serve.

We humbly repent before the Lord and ask the forgiveness of the body of Christ for inadequately representing Christ in our ministry, message, and methods. We have failed in diligently seeking to know His purpose and will. We have provided a ministry that has been a blessing to some but for others has opened a door to commercialism, focus on man and not on Christ and appealed to the flesh more than the spirit. We repent for criticizing both the public's apparent worship of the artists and of the artists' apparent unwillingness to confront this issue. We arrogantly blamed the problems, inherent in festival ministry, on everyone else, never allowing the Lord to turn His light on us. Our sins were ones of presumption and ignorance. We did not intend to mislead the body of Christ or bring offense to the name of Christ. Our hearts were for ministry, but our methods were misguided. Our encouragement to the body is to not take any ministry at face value, but be discerning of His Spirit, and of people's motives. Just because something or someone comes in the name of the Lord, there is no guarantee it is directed by the Lord. Sadly, we have been an example of that.

We have been encouraged by many to accept what the Lord is doing in our lives and return to the ministry of Jesus Northwest with new hearts and focus. Although the Lord is changing us, many problems still remain in the greater workings of the contemporary Christian music industry, the Christian publishing industry, and independent ministries we have worked with over the years. These issues prevent us from being involved with the type of festival we've been providing. We feel that within these industries and ministries much of what is done (e.g. ministry direction, decision-making, methods, even the message itself) is often driven by marketing - not the mind of the Lord. It is driven by analyzing demographics, not His anointing, by audio/visual production, not His power or presence. Money, success and business have become the bottom line. For a time we looked the other way and justified what was happening because ministry was taking place. But now, having been convicted of the same problems in our own lives, we know the Lord will no longer allow us to continue in this direction."

May God richly bless the people of Peoples Church (organisers of Jesus Northwest) for their faithfulness to Him and for following the convictions of their heart! And may the above also be an example to many others."

Randy Campbell was also later interviewed by Lindy Warren of The CCM Update, who wrote the following:

Campbell believes that ministry has taken place at the festival since its inception. He estimates an average total of 10,000 people have found salvation at Jesus Northwest. However, he speculated that "tens of thousands have been affected adversely. We've created an environment of worldliness and affected people in a negative way."

Campbell doesn't think the problems of sufficiency and pride he and his congregation are facing are exclusive to his church. He sees them in churches nationwide, in the Christian music industry and in writers and authors. "We're not trying to point fingers here. We don't feel like we've arrived, but we do have a responsibility to speak the truth. I do think ministries in general -- and festivals are a particular trap -- have to be dealing with many of these same specifics. This all comes down to asking, 'Is this about us, our desires, my vision?' "

He continued: "It's great that 800 lives are changed but the other 10 to 20,000 are coming away, saying, 'Isn't Jesus Northwest neat?' If they were saying, 'Isn't Jesus neat?' that would be okay, but they don't. We're impressing them with ourselves. If people walk away from an artist stage having more of an impression of man than Jesus, there's something wrong."

What is true of today's Christian music scene is also true of the book publishing scene. The following is taken from an article by Gene Edward Veith published in the Christian news magazine 'World' in July 1997:

"Visitors to the Christian Booksellers Association convention in Atlanta, July 14-17, will walk into the ultimate trade show. The latest T-shirts, plaques, CDs, and software will all be on display.

Celebrity authors will sign autographs. Bookstore owners will be feted at hospitality suites. Publishing insiders will schmooze and make deals. Last year's convention attracted 13,663 attendees, including 2,801 store representatives and 419 exhibitors from what has become, according to published reports, a $3 billion industry.

But such dramatic material success is not without its price. Today the largest Christian publishers are owned by secular corporations or have shares held by Wall Street investors. As ministries turn into big businesses, theological integrity can easily give way to marketing considerations...

The Christian marketplace thus follows the lead of the world's pop culture. A common saying in the industry is, Whenever a trend emerges in the secular arena, wait six months and a Christianized version will appear in the religious bookstores. Romances, horror novels, management books, and other popular genres that are essentially written according to easy-to-follow formulas rather than original insights all have their counterparts in Christian bookstores. Our culture's obsession with physical beauty gives rise to Christian diet plans and Christian exercise videos. Even when it comes to religion, Christian publishing often follows trends rather than leads, as in the rash of books on angels and near-death experiences inspired by New Age books on the same subjects..."

It is interesting to note the common industry saying quoted above: "Whenever a trend emerges in the secular arena, wait six months and a Christianized version will appear in the religious bookstores." This is certainly true of the Christian music industry also. If you have been into a Christian music store recently, or have listened to Christian youth radio, you may have noticed that the latest trends in secular music often have their Christian counterparts produced and marketed very soon afterwards. Thus, there is a continual flow of 'product', closely imitating the world, finding it's way onto Christian store shelves. And there is big money to be made from such a policy. For the executives know that many Christian kids, if they will not buy records by secular artists, can certainly be persuaded to buy the equivalent Christian ones.

The above may sound like a cynical comment, but the fact of the matter is that today the Christian contemporary music scene is a huge, multi-million dollar business. And it makes perfect business sense to create Christian "stars" (no matter what their personal walk with God is like) so that the Christian kids will still buy 'product' from the overall industry, one way or the other. Thus the music industry taps into the spending of all kids everywhere, from 'death metal' devotees to Christian fans of Amy Grant. Either way, the money still rolls in. And the modern Christian market is pretty easy to run, as well. To find a new artist, all you basically have to do is find a band that sounds like a Christian version of the latest secular bands, and market it to the Christian world.

What makes the Christian youth scene so easy to sell to these days, is the fact that there is an established Christian touring circuit (complete with promoters), Christian radio stations, Christian music magazines, and even large Christian music festivals. The whole scene is set up in a way that is very similar to the secular scene - in fact, almost identical. The problem with this is that the secular music scene is utterly corrupt by Christian standards - given over to "star" idolatry, materialism, spiritual laxness, and above all, the relentless pursuit of the almighty DOLLAR.

But has all this really had a deep affect on the Christian music industry? Absolutely! You only have to look at all the different media that fall into the Christian youth sphere these days to see how terribly secular everything has become. If you open many Christian youth magazines you will find album and concert reviews that just reek of cheap secular imitation - endless articles describing Christian music in terms of "dense, subterranean, swirling guitars" and "a sublime, soaring vocal assault", etc, etc. But almost nothing to describe the depth of the artists' Christian faith. (Ashamed to talk about it, perhaps? Not 'cool' enough? Or perhaps there really is no depth to the artists' spirituality?) In fact it is not uncommon these days to find entire Christian youth magazines in which you would have to look very hard to even discern that it is a Christian publication! An entire magazine full of the kinds of self-indulgent reviews quoted above, as well as interviews with Christian "stars" in which they often talk about Jesus very little, if at all. (Or perhaps it was edited out?) The style of the writing and the graphics certainly make the whole thing 'cool' in a worldly sense. But tell me, where is God in it all? And why are we so keen to hide Him?

Sadly, Christian youth Radio today is often not much different. In fact, I know of at least one Christian youth station that has a policy of not talking about Jesus hardly at all, but rather of letting the (often indecipherable) music do the 'ministering' for them. And so they will conduct on-air competitions to win snow-boards, etc, but very rarely will the name of Jesus ever be heard. (And I'm sure this station is not alone in this). Another 'cool' cop-out, I hear you say? Yes, it certainly does appear that many involved in Christian youth media these days are somewhat embarrassed by the 'Christian connection', and therefore spend an inordinate amount of energy trying to hide it. Poor Jesus! I wonder how long it's been since He had to put up with a generation of Christians who seemed so ashamed of being publicly associated with His name.

The effects of the Christian industry imitating the secular industry can also be seen in many other aspects of Christian music today. Christian bands are now routinely "hyped" in similar ways to secular bands (with writers and ad-men seemingly falling all over themselves to find glowing superlatives to describe the 'next big thing'). It is also noticeable that the "star" treatment, and the entertainment or 'party' factor involved in Christian music performance seems to be increasing (and this is being used as a selling point). The subtle pressure not to talk too much about Jesus or about deep spiritual issues seems to be growing also.

I would like to ask some fairly obvious questions at this point: Can anyone honestly imagine the apostles or any other New Testament ministries allowing (and even enjoying) the sick "star" treatment that is becoming so common today? And can you imagine them putting on a slick stage 'performance' that emphasizes their own place in the limelight rather than pointing to God? Can you imagine any of them bowing to the god of entertainment - striving primarily to entertain rather than to impart truth? Or trying so hard to be cool that they 'tone down' the spiritual content of their message? Finally, can you ever imagine any of the apostles charging money at the door before allowing people to come in and hear the gospel?

This last question raises a fundamental issue relating to much of Christendom today. For it has become very common, not just in youth concerts but in teaching meetings and seminars also, to charge people money just to get in the door. This never used to be the case. In fact, I would say that door-charges would have been almost unheard-of in Christendom up until about thirty years ago. This is because this practice undeniably runs right against the very spirit of the New Testament. For did not Jesus say, "Freely you have received; freely give"? (Mt 10:8). Can you ever imagine Jesus charging money at the door before people were allowed to come in and see Him? Of course not! What a ridiculous suggestion! Why then, do we Christians today feel that we can get away with charging people money in this way? Don't we realize that the very poor people whom Jesus welcomed will be kept away from our meetings simply because they cannot afford the price of admission? What a disgrace this is!

One of the major reasons this practice has sprung up in the church, of course, is that if you invite a travelling preacher to speak, then this way you can guarantee that you will at least cover costs and also provide the minister with a fair-sized 'purse' for his troubles. No need to take up an offering. The door-charge basically covers it. However, I have to say again that such a practice goes absolutely against the spirit of the New Testament, and against the clear instructions of Jesus to his followers. If the ministry is anointed, then people will gladly give, and thus the minister will be provided for. Why resort to charging people door-entry? I just cannot go along with this at all.

Apart from the costs involved, another reason why today's Christian events tend to charge an entry fee is because of the so-called 'entertainment value' of the event. Which of course brings us back to the heart of the problem that we have been discussing. Like John Blanchard (author of the book, 'Pop goes the Gospel'), I see the term "entertainment evangelism" as being a complete contradiction in terms. There is no such thing as entertaining someone into the kingdom (unless that kingdom happens to be Disneyland rather than the kingdom of God). As we have seen, true discipleship requires a deep and serious commitment. It is not a frivolous or lightly-taken decision. And we have also seen how severely the gospel itself can be affected by being combined with mindless entertainment. The pure New Testament gospel was never designed to be entertaining, but rather quite the opposite. It brings eternal issues to the fore. All entertainment tends to do is trivialize the issues involved. Thus, when trying to combine the gospel with entertainment it is almost always the gospel that suffers. However, it does not surprise me in today's climate that people are being charged for the 'entertainment value' of our Christian events. In fact, it says a lot about the actual content of such events, does it not?

It is my belief that today's Christian singers and bands must decide whether they are going to be entertainers or ministers. They cannot have it both ways. If they are going to be entertainers, let them simply entertain people and not pretend to be a Christian ministry. But if they are going to call what they are doing 'Christian' or "ministry", then they had better stop charging people money to come and hear them! "Freely you have received, freely give." This is the only way to operate if we are going to be truly serving Jesus in the public arena.

In saying the above about entertainment, etc, I do want to reiterate that there certainly is a very real place for music (including Rock music and other varieties) as a Christian art-form which expresses God's heart and also our own heart towards God. It is not the fact that such music is being used that bothers me, but rather the motivation, the approach and the 'heart' attitude of the music. (More on this later, including some of my own experiences).

Obviously, in speaking as I have about today's Christian music industry, I would not want to lump all those involved into one boat. There are hundreds of Christians around the world today who are employed by this industry, and many of them have only the highest motives for doing what they are doing. It has to be said however, that despite their own integrity and good intentions, there is much that is occurring in the Christian youth scene that is far from satisfactory. Similarly, of course, not all of today's music ministries have succumbed to worldly pressures and conformed to the shallow, 'cool' agenda. But sadly many have. Compromise, it appears, is fast becoming the order of the day.

One other major reason for this growing compromise - one which we have not yet discussed - is the "crossover" potential of Christian bands today. In other words, in the modern industry it is possible for a Christian artist to "crossover" into mainstream chart success with their music, and several of them have done so. But at what cost?

It is my belief that the Irish Rock band U2 has been one of the most important invisible influences on the Christian Rock scene over the last twenty years or so. (Though not so much now). It had been known in Christian youth circles from very early on that this exciting new band - the 'next big thing' was an almost-Christian band. (Three members were unorthodox though Spirit-filled believers, including front-man and lyricist Bono). I well remember their mid-eighties album 'War', with its veiled prophetic imagery. Jesus' name was even mentioned once (on 'Sunday Bloody Sunday')! It was a great record from many standpoints - one which they've really never equaled since (despite the later hype). And it was a hit album in the secular scene! Suddenly it seemed truly possible to be 'cool' in the eyes of the world and to have your Christianity too.

A lot of young Christian musicians suddenly sat up and took notice. And so did the industry in general. Subtle (half-hidden) Christianity sells records in the mainstream! The temptation to hide or submerge one's Christianity suddenly became very real for a lot of young Christian songwriters. After all, wasn't it better to gain widespread success by half-hiding your Christianity (and not preaching), than to stay overtly Christian and sell records only to

Christians? This was the great temptation. And many fell for it (including me, some years later). The whole concept of "crossover" (and compromise) had suddenly become very real and very tantalizing. And many of us were indeed willing to compromise our Christian lyrical content in order to gain secular success. This was when the word 'Jesus' began to be heard less and less amongst emerging Christian bands.

In the early 1990's, when my wife and I were founding our new alternative band, I was well aware of this whole crossover concept. And I knew that it was exactly the policy I needed to get us into the secular clubs. When it came time to write a new batch of songs for our band, I knew what I had to do. I made sure that what little 'Christian' content we had was so well hidden that the end result was that no-one ever knew we were Christians at all from our songs! And the most staggering thing of all was that I thought I was doing God a favor by covering everything up in this way. I honestly thought we had a better chance of reaching people for God by doing this. How blind and self-deceived we humans can be at times. Talk about "ashamed" of Jesus' name!

As I have recounted before, it took a series of unusual (though minor) disasters before I even slowed down long enough for God to get through to me that what I was doing was wrong. And it was only then that I could see what an incredible waste of time and effort it all was. This was not God's way! Compromising everything just to 'make it'. What on earth was I hoping to achieve? A profound sense of sorrow and conviction swept over me. And I knew I had to repent before God.

Sadly, it is my belief that there are huge numbers of young Christian song-writers out there today who have imbibed the same lies as I did. The Christian youth airwaves are full of songs that exude 'cool' and poetic cleverness, but how often do you hear something that sounds like it has come directly from the heart of one who walks very close to God? Where are the Davids of today - the searching, yearning spiritual psalmists and prophets of our generation? Could it be that they have submerged deep spirituality in favor of the shallow, popular limelight? It is my belief that we are currently paying a very heavy price for this "compromise and crossover" approach. For it has helped dilute everything about today's youth Christianity. As Jesus Himself said, "Whoever will be ashamed of me and my words in this adulterous and sinful generation; of him also shall the Son of man be ashamed, when He comes in the glory of His Father with the holy angels" (Mk 8:38).

This is not to say that I am against Christian songs making it big on the secular charts. In fact, I am all for it! (More on this later). But they must be openly CHRISTIAN songs, not half-hidden Christian subtlety, disguised as a secular hit. If we can't glorify God unashamedly, then we shouldn't be singing at all - that's my view now. And I'm afraid I'm no longer willing to compromise on it. However, this does not mean that I want to hear clichéd "Hallelujah, praise the Lord" lyrics every five seconds on Christian records just for the sake of it. While 'cool' guitar bands don't impress me much, I have to say that neither does the syrupy Nashville gospel sound so often heard on the older Christian stations. (Is it God who desires to have such insipid music representing His Son?) So no, I am not saying that we should fill our songs with trite "Praise the Lord" clichés. But what I believe we should be filling our songs with is an open, unashamed and deep expression of our heart towards God and His heart and calling towards us. And though it may be poetic, there really should be nothing 'hidden' about it.

Another aspect of this is that the old saying, 'The medium is the message' is often very true of music in general. In other words, the feel, the mood, and the type of music being used (the 'medium') very much impacts the overall "message" of the song, often even over-riding what the lyrics may say. For instance, if you try to marry joyful praise lyrics to a sad funeral dirge, people will be impacted more by the music than the lyrics, and they will conclude that it is a sad song. This is one very important aspect to music. The feel and the mood that it creates often say a lot more than the lyrics themselves. This is why I have serious doubts about certain types of modern music being suitable for Christian use.

For example, in recent years there has been a rash of angst-ridden, depression-inducing alternative bands that have become quite big in the secular music scene. (The lead singer of 1990s band Nirvana took this to it's logical extreme by blowing his head off with a gun). Death Metal and 'Screamo' also come to mind. Obviously this kind of musical feel is quite apt if all you want to do is promote mind-numbing nihilism, suicide or depression. But pray tell, what kind of Christian values or attributes are suited to such music? Is there any part of the Christian message or experience that could aptly be put across using such a sound? I have to say I seriously doubt it. (Unless it's a song about God being ignored and rejected. But even then, I doubt if it would sit right). And yet, isn't it true that there are Christian bands now trying to imitate these sounds?

Likewise, there are many secular bands today who play songs designed specifically to whip the crowd up into a frenzy of moshing and slam-dancing, etc. Can anyone tell me exactly what Christian values or attributes sit well with such music? Does mindless hedonism have any place in Christianity? I think not.

As I said before, with music it is often especially true that the 'medium is the message'. In other words, the sound and feel of a song usually say more than the lyrics themselves. The mood that is conveyed is the thing that usually speaks the loudest, and then the words of the song (in that order).

Thus, I believe that it is crucially important that we Christian songwriters today learn to match the Christian sentiments and message of our lyrics to a suitable musical feel. It is no good trying to meditatively worship God using thumping, driving music. But neither is it right to use quiet, thoughtful music when we are calling God's people to battle! I have to say that I also have real doubts that raunchy dance beats could be used to say anything with real spiritual depth. Some musical styles seem to lend themselves to shallowness and superficiality more than others.

These are extreme examples, but we need to be very aware as we are writing songs, whether the spiritual content of the lyrics is truly matched to the feel of the music. For too often this seems not to be the case today, and what Christian content there is, is often suffering because of the music it has been married up with. (And this is helping to "hide" its Christian aspect, also). Music is only ever effective if its sentiments and lyrics match its sound. (And I feel it is preferable for lyrics to be clearly audible, also). I will talk in more practical terms about this aspect later in the book.

In this chapter, we have taken a long, hard look at today's Christian music industry and some of the related media. The reason I believe this industry is so important is because for many young people it is the window through which they view Christianity and the gospel. And it also has a tremendous impact on the values and standards of young Christians. It helps advise them as to what is 'normal' amongst young people in Christendom, what is acceptable to God, and also what kind of attitude and behavior are likely to be rewarded in today's Christian world. Thus these media are now enormously important, particularly for our youth.

As we have seen, many aspects of the Christian youth industry today leave much to be desired from just about every standpoint. In fact, as I have stated, I believe the current situation to be a very real 'crisis', with repercussions that will have devastating results for many years to come, unless something drastic is done. I have no confidence at all that the Christian music industry is about to reform itself, except in a very superficial way. There is simply too much money at stake, and it is too easy just to live with the status quo. This is why I believe that God Himself is about to bring a great shaking and Reformation to this industry. For God makes it very clear in the Scriptures that He cannot live with a lukewarm church. And it is obvious that this particular industry is contributing significantly to the current lukewarmness found throughout Christendom. (Or perhaps it is just an exaggerated reflection of it?)

Right around the world in recent years, there have been continual prophecies given to praying Christians to the effect that God is about to visit great "shaking" upon His church and related institutions. As a writer who has specialized in studying past Reformations and moves of God, I would have to say that this is no idle threat. For God has moved with great suddenness and even ruthlessness many times down through history when lukewarmness has overtaken His people. He has torn down and He has built up. And I believe that today's situation is ripe for just such action. It does not surprise me that prophetic and praying people around the world are hearing the same things from God in this regard. Music industry, look out! For the time has clearly come, as has happened many times throughout history, for Judgment to "begin at the house of God" (1 Peter 4:17).

Chapter Five

IN THE WORLD BUT NOT OF IT

In his book 'Ashamed of the Gospel', John MacArthur writes: "Worldliness is rarely even mentioned today, much less identified for what it is. The word itself is beginning to sound quaint. Worldliness is the sin of allowing one's appetites, ambitions or conduct to be fashioned according to earthly values. 'All that is in the world, the lust of the flesh and the lust of the eyes and the boastful pride of life, is not from the Father, but is from the world. And the world is passing away, and also its lusts; but the one who does the will of God abides forever' (1 John 2:16, 17)... Yet today we have the extraordinary spectacle of church programs designed explicitly to cater to fleshly desire, sensual appetites and human pride - 'the lust of the flesh and the lust of the eyes and the boastful pride of life.'"

The remarkable thing today is that many young believers who have imbibed the "cool Christianity" ethos, wear gaudy worldliness almost as a badge of honor - a statement proclaiming, "Hey, we Christians are not nerds. We're hip. We're cool." They honestly believe that they are doing God a favor by representing Him in this way, and hence their desire to continually wear the latest 'hip' or alternative fashions and to follow the latest youthful trends. They feel that their worldly image is a vital part of their Christianity, and that it says a lot about them as people and as Christians. And they are right - it does. But perhaps not exactly what they intend.

So let's talk a little bit more about this sin of 'worldliness'. As I have said before, one of the most important (but little-realized) things about the whole 'cool' approach is that it greatly affects the content of the gospel or the 'Jesus' that we preach. It is very difficult to be 'cool' and at the same time to denounce sin as wrong, or to emphasize holiness, righteousness and 'taking up the cross', or to denounce pleasure-seeking, lust and covetousness. In fact, in creating a "cool" Christianity, we have to also create a whole new "Jesus" to fit in with our new image. For it is just simply not 'cool' in today's world to be uncompromising about sin or to call people to repentance. 'Cool' is the epitome of being conformed to the pattern of this world and the spirit of the age. You cannot be cool unless you conform to 'cool' expectations placed on you by the world. And this will affect absolutely everything (the way you talk, the way you walk, the clothes you wear, the music you listen to, and eventually even the way you think). One sure thing about being cool - it makes it VERY, VERY DIFFICULT to preach against worldliness or vanity (for these are part and parcel of its very essence!).

To be blunt, the simple fact is that trying to be cool goes utterly against the very spirit of the true gospel itself and every sentiment expressed throughout the Bible. 'Cool' is subtle pride. 'Cool' is overt worldliness. Is God cool? No, He can't be bothered conforming to the fashionable (frivolous and prideful) expectations of worldly men. And worldliness is roundly condemned throughout the New Testament.

I think many young Christians today would be shocked at what the Bible has to say about being conformed to the world. Speaking of true Christians, Jesus said: "If you were of the world, the world would love you as its own; but because you are not of the world, but I chose you out of the world, therefore the world hates you" (Jn 15:19). He also stated: "You are the salt of the earth: But if the salt has lost its savor, with what will it be salted? It is then good for nothing, but to be cast out and to be trodden under foot by men. You are the light of the world. A city that is set on a hill cannot be hid" (Mt 5:13-14). Notice what Jesus said about salt that has lost its savor. This is exactly what happens when Christians no longer use their influence for TRUTH, but rather conform to the world round about them. The 'salt' then becomes utterly useless, to God and to man.

The apostle John wrote these very incisive words: "Love not the world, neither the things that are in the world. If any man love the world, the love of the Father is not in him" (1 Jn 2:15). And the apostle James likewise wrote: "Do you not know that friendship with the world is enmity with God? Therefore, whoever wishes to be a friend of the world makes himself an enemy of God" (James 4:4). I don't think the Scriptures could be much clearer on this issue, do you?

Let me be very clear here: This whole "cool Christianity" thing is the complete opposite of the true gospel. As we have seen, the true gospel message involves "denying self, taking up the cross, and following Jesus." But this new gospel of 'cool' says, in essence, "indulge yourself, enjoy it all, look cool, be cool (carnal human pride in all its 'look at me' glory), and have God as well!" The true cross of Jesus speaks death to self, death to hype, death to pride and worldly 'cool', death to loving pleasures more than God. This is why the true gospel and the true message of the cross have always been "foolishness" to carnal man. They speak the OPPOSITE of worldliness - in fact, DEATH to the world! Surely the difference is very clear? ('Cool' is just another name for "pride", after all).

Having said all this, however, I do want to make it clear that we are not called by God to "separate" ourselves from the world. It is CONFORMITY to the pattern and mindset of the world that is the problem here. Jesus Himself ate with sinners and lived and moved amongst the common people of His day. But He never conformed to the spirit of the age in which He lived. He was truly "IN THE WORLD BUT NOT OF IT". He was in amongst it all, but He was not of the same spirit. In fact, He challenged the spirit of that age right to it's very face, so to speak. And He calls us to do the same in our day.

But does this mean that we are all to dress and act like straight-laced nerds? Not at all! But let's get the balance right. Let's forget about looking and acting 'cool', and start to concentrate on truly walking in the spirit of Jesus instead. Being cool is a very conscious and deliberate thing. It takes energy and effort (largely wasted). So let's forget about 'cool', and begin to seek a deep walk with God instead. Our clothes may be somewhat symbolic of who we are, but let's rather concentrate on God's concerns instead of worldly ones.

We have spoken before about the error that is currently flooding into the church in the name of "relevance" (trying to make our Christianity 'relevant' to the unchurched). The fact is, I am a great believer in "relevance" myself. But it must be a relevance that PREACHES THE ORIGINAL GOSPEL WITH IT'S ORIGINAL UNCOMPROMISING MESSAGE, using modern means. In other words, the gospel must remain as cross-centered, as convicting and as radical in it's demands as it was in the beginning, but the means of transmitting it may change (though never merely for the sake of being 'cool'). I actually believe that God can greatly use music, video and every other form of media (even secular television) to reach the lost, if we will co-operate with Him in doing it HIS way. And neither do I mind a certain amount of being "all things to all men" in order to reach the lost (after all, Jesus Himself came as a poor man preaching to the poor). But if our motive for this is to appear cool or 'hip'/alternative, or to appeal to the "God is fun" brigade, then I believe that we have gone way too far, and our bowing to the spirit of this world will greatly distort the message that we bring.

I hope you can see that I am by no means advocating some kind of strict, cloistered, "joyless" Christianity, or a return to the days of conformist conservatism in the church. What I am, in fact, advocating is a vibrant, relevant brand of the ORIGINAL NEW TESTAMENT FAITH – updated for the 21st Century, but full of the essence of everything that made the early church what it was. This is clearly the only way that we are ever going to impact this present generation with the life-giving power of the cross of Jesus Christ.

I believe in a Christianity that is truly 'liberated' and yet completely unpretentious and down-to-earth (rather than 'hip'-cool or 'party'-fun). A gritty, street-level faith - truly 'in the world but not of it' - reaching out to the man on the street, and utterly glorifying to God.

Probably more than at any time in history, we have a crying need today for searching, convicting 'repentance' preaching in our churches. The lukewarm church is in desperate need of some good, old-fashioned 'Revival' preaching on "sin, righteousness and judgment" (Jn 16:8). I do not believe that God can live with a compromised, pleasure-loving church. It is clear that today's Christians should be on their knees, begging God for forgiveness, not "partying up large".

In concluding this chapter, I just want to look at a simple question, which we have yet to examine in any real depth: This concept that Christianity has to be sold as a 'fun' party and God as a "cool" figure-head - where exactly does it come from? What exactly has occurred in the past twenty years or so that has caused many youth leaders to become so ashamed of the true, sin-repenting, historic gospel? (And in many instances the word "ashamed" is no exaggeration). Well, in my view, the fact is that the devil and the world have been absolutely whipping the church in skirmish after skirmish for the last thirty years or more. (With a few brief interludes, such as the 'Jesus' movement of the early 1970's).

The church's influence in the Western world today is only a fraction of what it was in the early 1960's and before. (Though, admittedly, Western society and the church of that era were overwhelmingly conservative). And it is still declining. This is one of the major factors, I believe, in what we are seeing amongst the youth today. We have been losing for so long that the subconscious approach seems to have become: "If you can't beat 'em, join 'em." In other words, you might gain more ground if you abandon your historic message (proven powerful though it is), and become more like the world (even 'cooler' if possible), so that you can attract the numbers in. A monumentally self-defeating attitude, if ever I heard one.

To me it seems very apparent that the church has been taking on more and more of the world's values, ethos and methodology over the last twenty years or so, to the point where shallowness and self-indulgence have literally reached epidemic proportions in many aspects of church life. We have invented for ourselves a safe, comfortable, convenient Christianity that bears almost no resemblance to the daring, self-sacrificing faith of the New Testament. Truly, in many ways we have become the epitome of the Laodicean church that was so sharply rebuked by Jesus in Revelation - the church that was described by Him as being "wretched and miserable and poor and blind and naked", but which described itself as being "rich and increased with goods, having need of nothing" (Rev 3:17). Sick, selfish, lukewarm church - do you not care that God has promised to "spew" you out of His mouth?

Compromise, ease and apathy are now clearly the order of the day in many branches of Christendom. (Despite all the "positive" talk about how wonderful and 'blessed' everything is in our churches). In fact you would have to say that our "gospel" today often seems to bear a closer resemblance to one of those body-machine infomercials on television (all smiles and glowing talk), rather than to the historic message of repentance and faith. But who cares about TRUTH anymore, so long as we've got ATTENDANCES - right?? As John MacArthur so eloquently states, it seems that "Burlesque is fast becoming the liturgy of the pragmatic church." We certainly know how to put on a good 'show' for ourselves these days, don't we? And many of us are now seemingly happy just sitting there, entertaining ourselves to death.

It is my strong belief that unless something drastic occurs, the future of genuine, historic Christianity is in grave danger, even within the space of the next thirty years or so. Things really have declined much further than most Christians are aware. The essential, piercing, bedrock truths of the gospel are now continually being eroded and deemphasized by a Christianity that seems to become more and more carnal with every passing year.

And unless we are having our ears tickled, it seems that many of us just don't want to know. Friends, when will the servants of God stand up and cry, "ENOUGH"??

Chapter Six

GENERATION 'X' - THE LOST CHILDREN

They have been called the first Post-Christian generation. Known by many names such as 'baby busters', twentysomethings, and "slackers", they have also often been described as the lost generation. They are an age-group that has grown up in the post-sixties spiritual and moral wasteland, where absolutes no longer hold sway and sexual permissiveness and the pursuit of pleasure are dominant philosophies preached incessantly from every blaring television and stereo. They are cynical, they are nihilistic, and it is hardly surprising that this is so. Born between 1963 and 1977, Generation X and their younger brothers Generation 'Y' often come across as bored and alienated, yet they hardly know why. But what is becoming clear is that what they are sensing and feeling is a direct result of the turmoil and selfishness that was brought upon the Western world through the cultural revolution of the Baby-boomers/Woodstock generation.

Please remember that I am writing this chapter as a Generation X-er myself, and so hopefully there will be some insights into the problems faced by my generation. I have also done quite a large amount of research into the causes and effects of the late-sixties cultural revolution in the West which was led by the Baby-boomers, and which has resulted in such spiritual devastation amongst the generations that followed.

It is widely acknowledged that Generations X and Y have grown up in something of a spiritual void - in an age widely regarded as postmodern and even as post-Christian. The AIDS epidemic, MTV, the mass drug culture, growing violence and permissiveness, and an entertainment industry that has become more efficient at selling 'rebellion' and alternative culture (by the truckload) each year - these factors have all left their mark. But even much of this falls into the category of 'symptoms' rather than root causes.

Possibly a little closer to the mark is the fact that Generation X are often the children of divorce, with 50 percent coming from broken homes. And as Christianity Today writer Andres Tapia points out, they are also the children of two-job families, where parents were often not around and the day-care center and the television set became the baby-sitters of choice, even from an early age.

In their book '13th Gen' (for the thirteenth generation to grow up under the U.S. flag), Neil Howe and Bill Strauss predict that because of their dysfunctional family background, X-ers will be jailed and executed at a higher rate than any previous generation in U.S. history. According to their statistics, every day 13 American youth commit suicide, 16 are murdered, 1,000 become mothers, 100,000 bring guns to school, 2,200 drop out of school, 500 begin using drugs, 1,000 begin drinking alcohol, 3,500 are assaulted, 630 are robbed, and 80 are raped.

What this has resulted in is a generation that is incredibly cynical and pessimistic about its future. A number of noted authors have written books that discuss this, including researcher George Barna, who authored 'Baby Busters: The Disillusioned Generation'. Little wonder that Richard Peace, professor of evangelism at Fuller Theological Seminary, calls this a "clinically depressed generation."

Because of their parents' unprecedented divorce rates, X-ers are often extraordinarily cynical about marriage and commitment. As Andres Tapia pointed out in Christianity Today, the median age for marrying has gone from 21 to 26 in the past four decades and continues to climb. Tapia also notes that: "Having grown up amidst headlines about fallen televangelists and crooked politicians, X-er trust in authority figures is low, and cynicism of anything organized, like the church and political parties, is high." Christian youth workers have even commented that when politicians or church leaders fall, X-ers aren't even shocked these days, for they have come to expect it. No wonder today's youth find cynical, irreverent and nihilistic TV shows so appealing.

The general pessimism and apathy amongst X-ers has led many Boomers to complain about "those spoiled slackers". They see the overwhelming desire amongst today's youth to escape, to party, to live for today and forget about tomorrow, as a cop-out caused by having everything handed to them on a plate. But what these Boomers are forgetting is that the X-ers have grown up in a far bleaker spiritual and moral wasteland than they ever had to contend with in their own youth. The Boomers decry the apathy, the drug-taking, the head-moshing and the music, but forget the role that the Baby-boomers themselves had in bringing-about this whole scenario. It is clearly the changed environment that the X-ers have grown up in that has largely caused them to become what they are.

To understand all this a lot better, it is time now to take a closer look at the cultural and spiritual revolution that occurred amongst the Boomer youth of the West forty years ago, and the causes and effects of it.

The period 1965 to 1969 were the watershed years of a massive youth revolution that completely altered our society's fundamental value system in almost every respect (much of it for the worse, as has now become clear). This revolution's philosophies have never been rescinded, and they still dominate much of Western thinking and values to this day. (Far more than most people are aware). In fact, it is in the area of spiritual beliefs, values and behavior that much of the most profound damage was done.

It is not difficult to trace the currents and influences that led up to this revolution, but it still astonished many observers at the time with its all-consuming nature and aggression. Although some of its roots go back centuries, the most logical place to start in briefly tracing this revolution's influences is probably in the latter half of the nineteenth century. In 1859 Charles Darwin published his famous "Origin of the Species", which promoted the view that man had evolved from apes. The atheists and humanists seized on this as an excuse to forever banish the concept of God as Creator and therefore Ultimate Judge of humankind. From around this time also, the church was being progressively weakened by a concerted attack on the veracity and inspiration of the Scriptures, both from without and within. The atheism of Bertrand Russell, the psychology of Freud, and the philosophy of Nietzsche, etc, all began to have a profound effect also. Humanism (the philosophy that 'man is the center of all things', rather than God) was just beginning its long climb toward complete dominance over Western culture. However, it was to be generations before the seeds sown during this period were to come into full flower.

In 1933, the American Humanist Association released its first Humanist Manifesto. Amongst the signers of this document was founding member John Dewey, a professor at Columbia University and probably the main author of the Manifesto. Dewey has been described as probably the most influential philosopher and educationalist in American history. Indeed, no-one has had more influence over the theory and practice of public Education in the United States in the Twentieth Century. In 1973, the American Humanists released an 'Updated' Manifesto, similar in sentiment to the first but this time much more detailed.

Contained in this second document were the following statements: "...traditional dogmatic or authoritarian religions that place revelation, God, ritual, or creed above human need or experience do a disservice to the human species... No deity will save us; we must save ourselves. We affirm that moral values derive their source from human experience... In the area of sexuality, we believe that intolerant attitudes, often cultivated by orthodox religions and puritanical cultures, unduly repress sexual conduct. The right to birth control, abortion and divorce should be recognized." Decrying dogmatic or 'preachy' religion, preaching Evolution as truth, stating that morals are to come from our own experience rather than from God, and promoting "tolerance" (that great humanistic buzz-word) so that we don't 'repress' perverse sexual behavior or ban abortion, etc - can you see how dominant such humanistic sentiments have now become in our culture? But this was not always so.

Those who actually called themselves 'humanists' were still a tiny (but Educationally influential) minority in the first half of the twentieth century. But there were many other currents that were flowing in exactly the same direction. And many of these streams were very strong. It gradually became more and more fashionable in intellectual and educational circles (i.e., the Universities and Colleges) to espouse liberal, humanistic philosophies. And it was from the ranks of these institutions that many leaders in medicine, teaching, law, sociology, business, politics and religion were drawn. Thus, the hidden philosophy of Humanism was already beginning to dominate the intellectual elite of Western Society. And it was they who were teaching the young ones.

Importantly, it was also from these liberal intellectual circles that the leading news editors, television producers, film directors and journalists were being drawn. So more and more, the output of the West's written, aural and visual media began to take on this liberal, humanistic slant also. And this had an enormous influence over time.

For those who would like further evidence that what I am saying is true, I would point you to several very well-researched books, such as those by Francis A. Schaeffer, plus 'The Closing of the American Mind' by Professor Allan Bloom, 'What is Secular Humanism?' by Dr James Hitchcock, 'The Battle for the Mind' by Tim LaHaye, 'The Neophiliacs' by Christopher Booker, 'Hollywood vs. America' by Michael Medved, etc, etc (There are dozens more).

It is important to remember that there were entire nation-states and trading blocs right around the world that were becoming officially 'humanistic' in their ideology during the first part of the twentieth century. (Which only goes to show how powerful these ideas had become over the last hundred years or so). I am speaking here, of course, of the socialist or communist states, inspired by the ultra-humanistic teachings of Marx, Engels, Lenin, Mao, etc. While this may appear at first to have had little effect on Western culture, the fact is that a milder form of these left-wing, humanistic ideals was percolating through many of the centers of higher learning in the West also. In fact, as I said before, it became quite fashionable amongst many intellectuals to espouse a liberal, humanistic ethos. (Though it is important to remember that Humanism is not so much a political stance as a social and spiritual one. It crosses most political boundaries).

And now, finally we come to the 1960's. While Humanism was already firmly ensconced in the West's institutions of higher learning, something truly earth-shaking would have to occur for this dominance to transfer to society at large. It was possible that gradualism might accomplish such a transformation over many decades, but in order for Humanism to become dominant fairly quickly, what it would take would be for an ENTIRE GENERATION to embrace this rebellious humanistic ethos. And this is exactly what occurred.

The 1950's had actually been a very conservative period in Western society overall (despite the rise of Elvis Presley and Rock 'n' Roll). "Harmless fun" was tolerated, but generally it was a time of strong family values. Divorce was relatively rare, abortion was almost unknown, and the drug culture - what on earth was that? Many went to church, and the West was fairly God-fearing (at least nominally). Tradition and hard work were held in high esteem, and the whole era was one of conservative family values overall. All this may sound rather dull, but most people knew how to let their hair down as well.

The children who were born in this period were dubbed the 'Baby-boomers'. They were largely the children of the servicemen and women who had returned at the end of World War II in 1945, and had embarked on an unprecedented wave of baby-making. The Baby-boomers (who became the 'hippy' youth of the sixties) were born in the late 1940's and 1950's, at the beginning of the most tremendous era of prosperity in Western history. Their parents had fought a war for their country, and now wanted to forget it all for awhile. They bought cars and homes. Their children were granted certain freedoms. And these kids were better-off than any previous generation. In fact, it could be argued that the cultural revolution that erupted a decade later was the luxury-child of spoilt kids who could only afford such a self-indulgent revolution because of the prosperity their parents had built. But perhaps that is being a little harsh?

There is no doubt that as they grew up, many Boomers came to regard their parents' generation as overly-conservative, materialistic and somewhat repressive. And obviously there is some truth in this. After all, their parents still remembered the hardships of the war years, and so had become unashamedly materialistic, with an emphasis on buying new "things" that would supposedly bring happiness. There certainly seemed to be a hypocrisy here. And there is little doubt also that much of that generation failed to pass onto their children any real depth of Christian faith or spirituality. This in itself was to have fateful repercussions not many years later. And it is also true that the rising tide of materialism was matched in the church by the growth of the 'prosperity' doctrine, which taught that it was OK for Christians to become rich (or at least well-off). In the minds of many, these kinds of hypocrisies helped to tie the church in with the upper middle-class 'Establishment' far more than should have been the case.

While there was certainly fairly mild Humanism taught in the secular schools from the 1950's onward (thanks in part to John Dewey's influence, no doubt), there was seemingly nowhere near enough to cause the massive revolution that followed. What happened in the 1960's was unprecedented and quite unexpected - a whole generation largely giving themselves over to this rebellious Humanistic philosophy almost overnight. (Of course they didn't call it Humanism. They termed it "throwing off the shackles of old-fashioned morality, tradition and God, etc." If it feels good, do it. Sleep with whoever you like, believe in whatever gods or non-gods you wish. 'Do your own thing!') What an amazing change - literally a "cultural revolution" which has essentially dominated the West ever since, whether many of us realize it or not.

There is no doubt in my mind that the revolution of the sixties was led by the musicians (the Beatles and the Rolling Stones in particular) and also by the new film directors and artists. "Change" was in the air right through the late fifties and sixties, but it didn't have to go anywhere near as far as it did. Unfortunately, REBELLION was also in the air. And the Beatles led the charge. (Though please don't think I am "anti" the Beatles. Actually, I love their music - particularly the early stuff, and I regard Lennon and McCartney as surely the greatest popular songwriting team of that century. But we have to realize how greatly they influenced the sixties youth to rebel, especially after 1965).

In the years 1965 to 1969 we find the genesis of today's mass drug culture, the modern New Age movement (the 'Age of Aquarius'), the modern satanism/witchcraft movement, the sexual revolution, the hyper-feminist movement, gay liberation, abortion on demand (legalized in England in 1967), etc, etc. And the musicians, artists and film-makers led the way in the acceptance of much of this. (Obviously the British bands were influenced by the San Francisco 'Acid' bands also).

Thus in the early sixties, we find The Sound of Music receiving all the acclaim and the awards, while by the late sixties we find Easy Rider and the Graduate acclaimed to the skies, and nudity and sex scenes becoming more and more common in hit films. And while in the early sixties John Lennon felt duty-bound to immediately marry his girlfriend Cynthia when she got pregnant, by the late sixties he could get away with simply leaving his wife and shacking up with his new girlfriend Yoko Ono, thus beginning a trend whereby 'living together' began to become the order of the day amongst young people. For those of us who weren't there, it is difficult to comprehend the enormous changes that came about in Western culture (particularly youth culture) over the space of just a few years. And these changes have had an enormous impact ever since.

Many people today look around at our world and the way it is heading, and they shake their heads saying, "What is going on? Was it always this bad? Why are things continuing to get worse and worse every year?" But they can't quite put their finger on where the decay comes from. Some just blame the media, others blame the Government. "Where did all this start?" Obviously, as Christians we can point to the Fall, and to the enormous tendency in humans towards depravity and rebellion. We can also truthfully point to the devil's hidden influence behind much of what we see. But in today's environment, I believe it is also important to point to the sixties as an example of what occurs when an entire generation give themselves to open rebellion, and the poison that seeps into the whole of society as a result.

Obviously, it was not just the Baby-boomer youth who were pushing this liberalizing agenda in the sixties. As stated earlier, there were already many intellectuals in the Universities and also in the media who were basically complete Humanists, and who supported the youth rebellion from the start. So the youth were not alone. But Humanism could never have become utterly dominant in the West so quickly without an ENTIRE GENERATION suddenly taking it on as their creed.

Some people (mostly Baby-boomers) claim that the youth of the sixties had only the most benevolent motives for doing what they did. They claim that all of their "causes" and their marches and sit-ins were done from quite pure motives. Others have admitted however, that the "causes" were mostly just an excuse to rebel - to 'give the finger' to the authorities and society's values. From all that I have read, I believe that for most of the youth, this was far closer to the truth. In fact, for many in that era, the whole revolution was just one big excuse to party: "Sex, drugs and Rock 'n' Roll". And it is their children who are paying for it all.

What happens when a whole generation overthrows every tradition they can lay their hands on? And what happens when they abandon God and basic morality in favor of selfish thrills and rebellion? As I have said, the rise of the modern New Age movement (new gods), the new sexual permissiveness (with the accompanying social disaster of mass fatherlessness and poverty-stricken solo mothers), the mass use of drugs as a lifestyle (along with gang wars for control of that drug market), divisive gender politics, etc, only became epidemics in our society after this period - 1965 to 1969. This was the watershed of the revolution. In fact, all the selfish, 'liberalizing' trends of the past thirty years (such as abortion-for-convenience) only became suddenly possible after that generation became aggressive campaigners for them. Since that time one could say that Rebellion has more and more become the Establishment.

There can be no doubt that 'Roe vs. Wade' (the court case that legalized abortion in the United States) just wouldn't have succeeded in the conservative America of the fifties and early sixties. But with a whole generation now 'liberalized', and many of the oldies kowtowing to them, every liberal in the land was making hay while the sun shone. Many new laws, including gender and abortion laws, could now be passed that never could before.

One notable bastion of Humanism over many decades has been the United Nations, and many UN resolutions which are now routinely signed into law by countries around the world are so humanistic and so 'politically correct' as to be sickening. The same is true of organizations such as 'Planned Parenthood'. (In fact, if you understand what the term "politically correct" means, then you will understand much of the basic thrust of Humanism. In many instances, Political Correctness IS Humanism outworked).

Fatherlessness (which amongst many urban blacks has now reached over 70%), permissive sex, gang violence and drugs existed before, but they only became epidemics after the sixties 'revolution'. And they have been destroying our society and our young ever since. The Boomers drank from their poison cup, and then they passed that poison on to succeeding generations. No wonder it just gets worse! "Situational" ethics, amorality, self-obsession, aversion to authority, and a massive vacuum in the area of spirituality (or has this been replaced by the "X-files"?!) - this is the legacy that has been left to today's young by the Woodstock generation.

I have to say that there have been few generations in history that have so willfully and selfishly left as an inheritance to their children a world that is so unimaginably worse than the world they themselves inherited. If we look at the statistics alone and compare the world of 35 years ago with our own, we can see that the Baby-boomers have succeeded in making this world pretty much a spiritual and moral "hellhole" for their children, in the space of just one generation. And all it took was mass selfishness, hedonism and rebellion (disguised behind slogans such as 'liberty' and "freedom"). But the party is over now.

The thing that staggers me the most is that there seems to be almost no recognition today of the root causes and the reasons behind many of the West's problems. (Perhaps certain parties do not want to admit the truth? Maybe they prefer the old line: "We were simply idealistic youth, making the world a better place"?) But slowly the truth is filtering out. If you ever get a chance to read a 1996 book by renowned Social Scientist David Popenoe entitled "Life without Father", you will see how clearly the results of the last thirty years are showing up statistically. And Michael Medved's "Hollywood vs. America" is similarly incisive, from the point of view of examining the invasive sickness afflicting much of our mass media and popular culture from the 1960's onwards.

As you can see, every one of the basic planks of Humanism are now utterly dominant in our Government, our media and our Education system. And for many of us, they have long become dominant in our minds also. For they have been preached incessantly (but often unnoticed) by just about every television program, every news bulletin, every UN declaration, and every modern school program over the last thirty years. And in many cases, the church has been worn into the ground by this propaganda bombardment, to the point where the Christians have literally become "ASHAMED OF THE GOSPEL", and are now trying to 'dress it up' to make it fit in with Humanism a little better. What an enormous revolution it would take now, to turn all this around.

One of the most obvious results of the dominance of Humanism is its enormous undermining effect on the family unit. The damage that this has caused has lately become so clear that even those who used to be notorious for their attacks on the family have now become strangely silent. The devastation is everywhere, for all to see. What happens when you make it easy for men to father a child and then to simply skive off and do the same with another partner? And what happens when you liberalize the divorce laws, allowing similar scenarios to occur even with married couples? What happens when Feminism strips men of respect, authority, responsibility and position, accusing them until they feel even more marginalized within the family unit? And what happens when Feminism hints that women can do a better job of raising kids without dad around? (A disastrous, proven lie). The result of all this is an epidemic of fathers leaving their partners and children, creating a situation where hundreds of thousands of children are growing up entirely without their own fathers in an increasingly harsh world.

Statistics clearly show that solo mothers and their children today (like throughout history) are almost always trapped in poverty. Their children are far less likely to do well at school or to gain a degree at a College or University. In other words, a cycle of poverty is being created. And there is overwhelming statistical evidence that girls who are raised without their own father are many times more likely to become pregnant outside wedlock themselves (in other words, the poverty cycle claims further victims). Boys who are brought up without their father are statistically far more likely to be unemployed, poorly educated, and to become involved with gangs, etc. Boys especially need the authority and discipline of a father in the home. In fact, huge statistical studies have now clearly demonstrated that fatherlessness in itself is such a massive social disaster that it is probably a leading cause of many of the West's social ills. (Again, see 'Life without Father' by David Popenoe). In fact, the 70% plus fatherless rate in many urban black communities is without a doubt the leading cause of many of the terrible gang problems found in those areas. This is now widely recognized by many sociologists and activists (though shouldn't the warnings have gone out thirty years ago?)

In a relatively God-fearing society, where divorce, adultery and sex outside marriage are frowned upon, and where there is respect for fatherhood and for authority in general, it is very difficult for society to become as fractured and sick as Western society has become. In fact it is almost impossible for the rot to get so deep. But when you throw away your belief in God and create your own morality, then you are on the slippery slope to disaster. It has now become even more obvious than ever that God created the family to be the basic building block of society, and if the family unit is sick, then society itself becomes sick. The fabric of our society today is unraveling because the family unit is falling apart. What has occurred over the last thirty years amounts to a gleeful and concerted attack by the humanists and liberals against the family unit, both through the media and through our Education system; and even using legislation. (Though the media has proven to be the most important propaganda tool of all).

Of course, in the eighties the Baby-boomers suddenly went 'straight', and many could suddenly be found wearing suits, driving late-model cars and even trading stocks and bonds. While some may think this represents a significant transformation, actually beneath it all little has changed. The humanistic lies that became dominant in the 1960's have never been dethroned, and still dominate our culture, probably more now than ever. The fact that the Boomers populate corporate boardrooms these days rather than protest marches has made little seeming difference. If anything, it has made these lies even more powerful. Many Boomers themselves have freely acknowledged that the changes that occurred in the eighties were more for pragmatic, self-serving reasons than anything else. It was time to make some money and set themselves up financially. In fact the generation that had been dubbed the "Me" generation - the one that had popularized the terms 'self-concept', self-realization, self-esteem, self-image, etc - was simply running true to form. "SELF" was indeed the motivation for much of this lifestyle change. But Humanism still rules the West. And in fact the Boomers, who are now in their forties and fifties, are now in positions of power in many spheres, including the media, politics and education.

And the sleazy movies encouraging teenage sex, the suggestive songs and music videos, the rebellious, anti-authority TV shows, etc, just go on and on, getting worse and worse every year.

Is it fair, though, to point the finger at one particular generation - even a rebellious one? Yes, I think so. After all, Jesus did in His day. It is my genuine belief that you would have to go back centuries to find a generation that has caused anything like such devastation just through their own selfishness, hedonism and rebellion. Usually it takes a war or some terrible cataclysm to produce such nightmarish results in following generations. But what exact purpose does it serve to point to one particular generation in this way? Well, it is my strong belief that God is calling many Boomers to real repentance for the part they have had in this revolution (or even in acquiescing to it), and for the legacy that they have left for their children. I also believe that, as the old saying goes, "Those who have not learned the lessons of history are bound to repeat them". The fact is, we just cannot afford to ignore or gloss over what happened forty years ago, and neither should we shrink back from telling it like it is. Not only must we learn the lessons so we don't repeat them, but it is also up to us to root out and deal with the lies and the devastation that are still with us today. If we don't know exactly where they came from, then we will find this enormously difficult.

Sadly it is my belief that the selfish revolution of the Baby-boomer generation is bringing judgment upon the entire Western world.

And in a sense, the children "to the third and fourth generation" are likewise under a curse because of it. It is also my belief that the overwhelmingly Laodicean state of today's church can be attributed to many of the same causes. May God help us all.

It is important to remember, however, that there are many amongst the Baby-boomers themselves who do not (and perhaps never did) hold to the errors of their peers. Many Christians, even from that age-group, opposed the selfish and destructive changes that were taking place. God always has His "remnant" from every generation. So we certainly cannot tar everybody with the same brush. And it is also important to remember that the Baby-boomers are not necessarily the PARENTS of Generation X. (Many are the parents of Generation Y). The X-ers are, in fact, the generation of youth who followed directly after the Boomers, but they are not necessarily their children. Thus many X-ers (including myself) are not speaking against their own PARENTS when they are speaking of the Woodstock generation. (I thought this was an important point to make).

I have to say that I have found some definite hope for our generation in the Scriptures that speak of a great end-time Revival, just prior to the return of the Lord Jesus Christ. One passage is particularly noteworthy in this regard: "Behold, I will send you Elijah the prophet before the coming of the great and dreadful day of the LORD: And he shall turn the heart of the fathers to the children, and the heart of the children to their fathers, lest I come and smite the earth with a curse" (Mal 4:5-6).

It seems that those who are to arise with this 'Elijah' calling in these last days will have this as a vital part of their mandate. The parents must be called to repentance for what they have done to the children, and the children must deal with their rebellion repentantly, and embrace and honor their parents. Any refusal to do so from either side will result in God's "curse". What an enormously important task! I pray that it will not be long before we begin to see such ministries arise, for they are certainly sorely needed in our day.

Something God seems to have been speaking about to a number of people is the need for the Christians of Generation X to become true spiritual 'fathers' to Generation Y. It is felt by many that amongst the Boomer generation of Christians, there have been relatively few who were willing to be true spiritual 'fathers' to the young. Plenty of leaders, but not enough fathers. The thing about fatherhood is that it often involves consciously taking the hard road rather than the easy one. A father has to take RESPONSIBILITY for the young ones under his charge. The buck truly stops with him. He will be held accountable for them, and HE HAS TO ACT LIKE IT and make the hard decisions and speak the hard words where necessary. It is often the father who is the disciplinarian of the family (though administered only out of love and desire for the best, of course). Paul told Timothy to: "reprove, rebuke, exhort with all longsuffering and doctrine" (2 Tim 4:1). A true father is not tyrannical or repressive, but he is certainly a man of true (not false) authority. And he must also be a man of sacrificial, fatherly love for his children. He must be strong but tender at the same time, looking always to challenge and progress his children, and to see them develop. Today, we have a stunted, apathetic church, full of gifted people who never get the chance to develop their giftings. I have to ask the question: Would true fathers allow such a thing?

I believe there is a real warning in this for Generation X also. It is all very well discussing the shortcomings of what we see all around us. But are we ourselves willing to take on the challenge? Are we willing to become true fathers to Generation Y? This is the big question that faces all of us in Generation X, I believe.

I realize I have been very direct in this chapter, and I have run the risk of offending some readers. However, I hope you can accept that it was not my intention to offend anyone, but rather to discuss very openly and candidly many of the problems that we face and the origin of them. Please be aware that I have no personal axe to grind in this (I was not born or raised by Baby-boomers, for instance), and I really do not feel that I can be accused of any kind of bias. I have spent a great deal of time researching this topic, and have read widely on the social and cultural aspects of the 1960's. And I have to say that everything I have read has drawn me toward the same conclusions.

It should now be obvious that many of the negative characteristics of Generations X and Y have resulted from profound changes in our society over the last 35 years or so. The challenges that confront us in dealing with these problems are by no means superficial. Rather, they stem from roots deeply embedded in the very fabric of our society itself. In the chapters to follow I will be looking at ways in which I believe God would have us fight and win the war for the hearts and minds of Generations X and Y. It is my hope that eventually, through repentance by both the young and the old, there will come a deep reconciliation and understanding between all generations in the church, plus a determination to fight and win for God's cause together. And it is my prayer that in the near future, the situation in regard to Generations X and Y will not appear anywhere near as hopeless as it does now. But things must change very radically if we are to see anything like real victory. And that is what the following chapters are all about.

Chapter Seven

THE DOMINANT LIE

As we have seen, there are a number of Humanistic lies that utterly dominate the spiritual landscape of the West today. But towering over them all are the core lies that in many ways have pulled the rug right out from under the true gospel in this modern age. The question I would ask at this point is: Which is the one dominant, over-riding LIE that the devil has sold the Western world in the last thirty years or so, that most hinders men and women from coming to repentance? And could it be that if this particular 'Dominant Lie' is uprooted and destroyed, then the way will be cleared for massive Revival?

I certainly believe that if the most powerful of these 'strongholds' (which one could call "dominant lies") can be attacked and brought down, then a massive harvest will result. But which exact lie is the most destructive? Well, the following are some of the conclusions I have reached: As a man who wrote to me recently said, it seems that we can no longer preach "sin" these days, because many young ones hardly know what Sin is any more. There is a very significant and disturbing level of truth in this. (And of course, this in itself totally strips the gospel of its historic power). In fact, I am convinced that this is the one over-riding Humanistic doctrine that most undermines the true gospel - the fact that the Biblical concept of 'Sin' is no longer widely held or understood.

A lot of Christians these days might be surprised to know that in the New Testament, and virtually throughout church history (until recent times), the thorough preaching of REPENTANCE FROM SIN was an integral part of the gospel. But we almost never hear such preaching now, do we? In fact, these days we seem to have invented a friendly, "positive" (in the marketing sense) 'toothpaste commercial' of a gospel, in which sin is mentioned rarely if at all (it is certainly not thoroughly discussed). Our gospel today more often resembles one of those pep-talks given by the big-time 'motivational' speakers who populate the after-dinner circuit, than the repentance message of the Bible. It may be full of jokes, illustrations and anecdotes, but it rarely cuts as a double-edged sword to the heart. We have unconsciously allowed the spirit of this world to dominate our preaching. What fatal compromise! And the results of such "gospel" preaching are seen throughout Christendom today.

For some years now I have been studying and writing on past Reformations and Revivals. And if it is one thing that characterizes true Revival preaching down the ages, it is the EXPOSING OF SIN AND THE PREACHING OF DEEP REPENTANCE. Probably the most outstanding and well-known American Revivalist, Charles Finney, was a great expounder on repentance from sin. So was Wesley. So was Whitefield. So were Edwards, Roberts, Sung, Goforth, Savonarola, Luther, Knox, Spurgeon, Booth, etc, etc. (In fact, Wesley said that he preached "90% law and 10% grace" - in other words 90% conviction of sin and 10% God's mercy and salvation. Such a ratio was not uncommon amongst the best of the Revivalists. These guys were truly REPENTANCE preachers!). And these men were responsible for the salvation of multiplied thousands of souls, and for huge movements that sometimes spanned the globe. If we look at the Bible, we see that Jesus Himself was a repentance preacher, as was John the Baptist, plus all of the apostles. So why do today's preachers suddenly feel that they can invent a better, more "positive" gospel? Convenient compromise wouldn't have anything to do with it, would it?

The fact is, the Bible is very clear that the Holy Spirit comes to CONVICT people of "SIN, RIGHTEOUSNESS AND JUDGEMENT" (Jn 16:8). Note that the Holy Spirit does NOT come to convict sinners that Jesus will make them 'happier' and enable them to 'feel fulfilled'. (This is what toothpaste commercials are trying to convince us of). So why on earth have we stopped PREACHING 'sin, righteousness and judgment', when this is the exact thing the Holy Spirit wants to convict people of? Why are we toning our message down, to 'tickle the ears' of our hearers? (Thus stripping the gospel of much of it's historic power). It has been truly said that we don't preach the old "rugged" cross these days, but rather a smooth and easy Hollywood version. Is it really the 'narrow' path that we are having our new converts embark on today, or simply a religious version of the old 'broad and easy way' that leads to destruction? For the Bible makes it clear that lukewarm disciples are no disciples at all. Where is the denying of self and the taking up of the cross to follow Jesus?

Instead of convicting people of their sin these days, it seems that we would rather woo them in with promises of happiness and an improved lifestyle. But since when has such a message ever produced RADICAL DISCIPLES of Jesus? Thus, as the music gently plays during our altar calls and every eye is closed (lest we 'scare' the poor converts away), one almost never hears an appeal these days based on how desperately sinners need to get rid of their sin, but rather on how their life can be improved. So, in essence, it is for SELFISH motives that we are asking them to come in, rather than because they have offended an Almighty God (the Judge of all the earth) with their sin. "Easy-believism" has truly become the order of the day. And how perfectly this all fits into an age when Humanism and the selfish pursuit of happiness rule. It is clearly the world's ethos that is now dominating our gospel, rather than the other way around.

As we have seen in the previous chapter, in the Humanistic revolution of the sixties, "Sin" as a concept was virtually abolished (particularly amongst the youth). Moral absolutes were thrown out. Everything became no longer black or white, but varying shades of grey. "Be happy, feel free, do what you want, cast off the shackles of outmoded morals and values. Do what you feel..." etc. And so it still is today. A completely 'non-judgmental' (i.e., no right or wrong) approach to everything. So long as you don't "hurt" anybody, you can do as you please. You can sleep with anyone (of any sex), you can abort your babies, you can taste any pleasure, you can believe in any 'god' (including yourself). Today the worst sin you can be accused of is being "judgmental". ('How dare you apply your value system to ME? How dare you call what I'm doing "wrong"??') 'Tolerance' is the great buzzword, and anything else is "bigoted ignorance". We have already seen what disastrous consequences such a philosophy has created in today's society.

In many ways, the Biblical concept of 'Sin' has now almost ceased to exist in many people's thinking and beliefs. Now this has enormous implications for the preaching of the true Gospel. (The devil must be laughing his head off, at the way he has been able to pull the rug out from under our message). For if you wipe out the concept of 'Sin', then you wipe out a massive part of the basic gospel itself. FOR THE ONLY REASON JESUS NEEDED TO COME WAS TO DEAL WITH MEN'S SIN. If there is no consciousness of Sin, then the true gospel ceases to make any sense. Why do I need forgiveness? Why do I need to repent? Why did Jesus die in the first place? The cross is made of NO EFFECT without a consciousness of Sin. This is why all the great Revivalists emphasized Sin, and the only remedy - Jesus. If you feel you have little sin, then you will feel little need of Jesus. And then the gospel is severely undermined. The devil knows this. He has seen many Revivals, and he knows if he can stop people becoming convicted of their sin, then he can stop them from responding to the gospel in significant numbers. Why do you think there is hardly any conviction of sin amongst today's generation? Because in the previous generation, the whole concept of it was virtually abolished (and still is). It's as simple as that.

Now, if we wish to see massive Revival amongst today's generation, what is the first thing we need to do? REFUTE THIS DOMINANT LIE. And if we can't go back and prove that it was wrong to abolish sin - prove that it has done untold damage - then it is surely very difficult to refute. For it is ingrained into the very fabric of today's society. And our youth have it ingrained into them also. But if, under the anointing of God we can show them the terrible harm it has done, then it is possible to refute the lie, and to re-introduce and preach the concept of "sin" again. Thus the whole, powerful gospel would begin to make sense once more.

It may sound strange to some, but it is clear to me that real preaching on 'Sin' will not work with today's youth unless some attempt is made to show that the concept of Sin itself actually does make sense, and that it was harmful and wrong to abandon it. To many of today's youth the Biblical concept of Sin is now so foreign that I am convinced that they will not comprehend it unless we give them good reasons to do so. And I feel that going back and refuting the 'dominant lie' is probably the best way of accomplishing this. I am convinced that the Holy Spirit can be blocked from convicting people, unless they have a basic concept of what Sin actually is.

As previously stated, I have studied church history for many years, and I am well aware of the level of conviction of sin needed for people to repent in large numbers. No consciousness of sin - no Revival. It's as simple as that. For what is there to repent of? The gospel almost entirely loses its power without this. (Not to mention the concept of "holiness", which is another term that has become strangely unfashionable in today's church). What the devil did in the late sixties was to pull the rug out from under us. We have no "foundation" from which to preach the true gospel in power any more. However, I am convinced that this lie can be refuted, and we can begin to win again. But only if we dare to tell it like it is.

Why do I feel that we need to expose the wrongness and error of the sixties revolution to destroy this lie? Because it was in those days (the late sixties) that this lie truly became dominant, and we can see the fruit of it by looking at what occurred then and why. What were the results of throwing away all morality and restraint? What were the results of 'free love' and "if it feels good, do it"? It is there for everyone to see. And this will lead people to see the sense in preaching against Sin. For they will see what the world became like without it. The whole concept of 'Sin' will make sense to them once more. And this will open them up far more to the convicting power of the Holy Spirit.

I am convinced that only if this dominant 'Stronghold' in people's hearts and minds is attacked, that real Revival preaching and a great outpouring of God's Spirit in the West can be expected. I believe that at present, this lie is holding back many Westerners from believing the true gospel. I can't stress enough how important I believe this attacking of the 'Dominant Lie' is. It really could be one of the major keys to Revival in our generation, I believe.

There has been some talk in recent times of the possibility of a coming 'right-wing' wave - a massive reaction to the liberalization and the sickness of our society over recent decades. I am one who believes that such a reactionary wave is a definite possibility, and that it could pose enormous dangers to our society. For such a wave would not merely undo some of the damage of liberalization. It is likely that it would also bring power to extremist right-wing elements in our society, particularly amongst the youth.

Some may think that this is a far-fetched scenario. However, all the signs are there right now, pointing to the likelihood of such a wave. For instance, in European countries we are currently seeing the rise of a number of neo-Nazi, skinhead and racist groups, which are steadily growing in popularity. The same is true in Russia, where a right-wing strongman commands considerable popular support. In the United States, extreme right-wing 'militia' groups are on the rise, with many young people becoming drawn to them. And the fundamentalist Moslem movement (the 'million-man march', etc) is also gaining enormous popular support amongst Afro-Americans.

There is also a huge groundswell in the West against the extremes of 'Political Correctness', and PC-mockery is now quite common. What a lot of people don't realize, of course, is that in reacting against Political Correctness, they are often reacting against Leftist Humanism, which is the source of much of this PC ideology. Naturally, none of this has had much of an impact (yet) on the actual strongholds that Humanism has in most of our leading institutions. But the fact that such sentiments are bubbling just under the surface throughout much of the West should give us pause to think.

Of course, a lot of this has resulted from the open sickness and decay afflicting Western society. Every day, the television news brings an ever-more graphic assault to our eyes and ears showing a Western society out of control. (Murders, suicides, rapes, mass-shootings, drug-wars, etc - it just gets worse and worse). Leftish Humanism has indeed reaped a bitter harvest on our streets. And many average people are also thoroughly sick of the continual bombardment of ever-cheaper, and gaudier SEX that is being pumped into young, unsuspecting minds today. I tell you, a 'cultural revolution' against all this is not at all unlikely. In fact, many of the right-wing groups that are already on the rise are being fuelled by the depraved moral sickness infecting our society. People are just so tired of it all. And they are joining the groups (violent and misguided though they be) that are actively militating against this sickness.

Now the dangers of all this should be obvious. It was just such desperation that saw right-wing extremists such as Hitler and Mussolini rise to power. No-one should ever under-estimate the potential of such massive swings of public sentiment. And I truly believe that such a massive reactionary wave is on the way, particularly amongst today's youth. But on the brighter side, it is my belief that this wave - even if it is milder than I think it will be - will be our one opportunity to gain back the high ground from the enemy, and to see widespread Revival amongst the youth. (That is, if extremist political elements do not seize control of it, and push the whole thing far to the fascist, reactionary right). The key will be who will be most effective in harnessing and channeling this wave. With God's help, let it be us!

It is clear that the West is in desperate need of true Revival today, and I am convinced that any such Revival must take advantage of the prevailing spiritual and social conditions of the hour. The reason the Leftist / Humanistic revolution of the sixties was so successful was because the time was right, and society was ripe for such massive change. Reaction and Revolution were in the air, and the liberal activists were able to push their agenda further than they had ever dreamed possible in a very short time. The same was true of the spiritual impact of that revolution. As I said before, the activists of that period certainly knew how to make hay while the sun shone.

But the same has to be true of us Christians today, if we are ever going to see the spiritual situation in the West turned around. I am convinced that the coming Revival will come in with a wave of "anti-liberal" sentiment that is already building around the world. But if the Christians fail to take advantage of this wave, then obviously violent and extreme elements will be very willing to do so. Of course, such a wave in itself will accomplish nothing unless we use it to point people to the cross of Christ. Left-wing or right-wing in themselves mean nothing to God. It is the cross of Christ that saves. But if there is a wave of sentiment sweeping the globe that we can use to point people to the cross, then we would be foolish not to do so. What we are looking at is a kind-of 'sixties' revolution, but in the opposite direction (i.e., towards conservative or even 'Biblical' values rather than permissiveness). But there is clearly great danger in such a volatile situation also.

Of course, the devil is very aware of all this, and he is an expert at using such 'revolutionary' swings of sentiment. This is how Hitler got into power, after all. Left or right, it matters little to the devil so long as he is in charge. He will happily ride a fascist tide, just as easily as he will ride a permissive one. In fact, in the West at present, it is probable that the devil would prefer a right-wing revolution, because it may result in widespread violence and upheaval, and possibly even persecution against true Christians, etc. It is the extreme ideologies (Communism on the left and Fascism on the right) which allow the devil to inflict the most excessive destruction on people and society. (In fact, right now it is quite possible that the devil is deliberately pushing society to real extremes of leftish Humanism and permissiveness, just so that the reaction back the other way will be as violent and extreme as possible when it comes. This really is something to be aware of).

But as I have said, the coming 'philosophical revolution' in the West is a golden opportunity for Christians to seize the moment and for God to move mightily around the world. Such moments usually come only once or twice in an entire generation. If the Christians "seize the day" and use the tide that is turning against permissiveness and Political Correctness to point to Jesus Christ and His Truth, then there can be a great harvest (particularly amongst the young) around the world. But woe betide us if we miss such a golden opportunity.

We live in a sin-sick world today - rapidly tiring of sleaze and violence, but not quite sure what coherent alternative there might be. The tide has been turning for some time, but I believe that the wave that is coming will be far more violent than most people realize. Unless the Christians channel and harness this wave, then a form of right-wing extremism could well take hold. We live in truly dangerous times, and unless God can find 'men and women of valor' to stand up for His Truth at this time, then we will deserve everything we get.

I have pondered all this a great deal over the last few years, and I am convinced that this wave is not far away. Already these sentiments are bubbling everywhere just below the surface. But as yet there is no coherent 'movement' to give voice to these sentiments in a down-to-earth way. The devil would love to provide just such a movement at the right moment, if the Christians cannot. (He will point to reactionary politics as the answer, rather than Christ). I am convinced that even today's jaded and cynical youth will respond to a real CHALLENGE and will rally to a cause that is truly worth fighting (and dying) for. But we in the church today are failing to provide such a cause. Friends, this has to change, and it has to change FAST.

I believe that God is granting us one (last?) enormous opportunity. And what fools are we, if we let it pass us by. There has probably never been a time when the old saying about "seizing the day" has been more applicable to the Christian church. But if we think "preachers in suits" are going to reach the youth of this generation, then we must be out of our minds. Truly, great daring and boldness are required. Tell me, friend, will you rise to the tremendous challenge that confronts us?

Chapter Eight

THE COMING STREET-REVIVAL

The year 1878 saw the birth of one of the most outrageously radical, zealous and anointed Revival movements in the history of the church. I am speaking, of course, of the early Salvation Army, which for its first thirty years was one of the most extreme, unusual and effective Christian movements that the world has ever known. Made up mostly of young zealots and led by a spiritual dynamo named William Booth, this was God's answer when extreme measures were called for to combat the apathy and spiritual torpor of the times. And there can be little doubt that we live in such times again today.

Originally named simply the 'Christian Mission', Booth's organization always had a 'Revival' feel about it. But it wasn't until they went military in 1878, with flags, battle songs, war uniforms, etc, that the whole thing exploded worldwide. Booth himself became the Army's first General. This was no longer simply home-missionary work. It was holy guerrilla warfare against darkness and the devil. Booth's motto was: "Go for souls and go for the worst". It was nothing less than all-out war.

Within five years of becoming a military-style 'Army', Booth's fifty mission stations had become 634 corps (106 of them overseas). And his soldiers were some of the most innovative, daring and war-like disciples of Jesus that had ever walked the earth. There was much opposition. In the year 1882 alone in England, 669 Salvationists were physically assaulted, 56 Army buildings were wholly or partially wrecked, "skeleton armies" of local toughs were formed to attack the Salvationists, and 86 Salvation Army soldiers were thrown into prison for causing a disturbance on the streets. There were literally street-riots almost everywhere they went. And they were front-page news around the world. In the several years that followed, things only got wilder. In the year 1884 alone, no less than 600 Salvationists were arrested and imprisoned in England by the authorities.

The Army always maintained that it was a restriction of religious freedom to deny them the right to hold their marches and open-air meetings. And they would gladly go to jail in defense of the right to proclaim the gospel on the streets. In fact, they would usually refuse to pay even the smallest fines on principle, and so jail was inevitable. But they always held a huge, raucous march to and from the prison on behalf of the arrested soldiers. And, as a New Zealand Salvationist declared after one such occasion, "The whole town was stirred up. The Army got properly advertised, souls were saved, money rolled in, and God's name was glorified." An exasperated Court Judge once advised another contingent of arrested soldiers "to read and meditate on their Bibles a little more, to talk less, and to trust less to the hideous clamor of drums and brass instruments. Drums and trumpets were fit accompaniment for a circus, but out of place on Sunday in a quiet town like Milton." It has to be said that such advice had little noticeable effect.

As I have said, the Salvationists were well-known for their rather raucous brass band music (which was the loudest street-music around at the time) and their anointed, fairly blunt and down-to-earth preaching on the streets. It was quite common for them to form brass bands out of instruments held together by bits of string, and with musicians who could hardly even play. One eyewitness described the noise emanating from one outfit as sounding "like a brass band that has gone out of its mind". They often used the popular drinking songs and pub songs of the day, changing the words to make them into battle hymns or worship songs. As William Booth said, "Why should the devil have all the best music?" (A saying also credited to Martin Luther and John Wesley before him). The early Salvation Army were truly outrageous by the Victorian standards of the day - in fact by any standards. But while respectable church people were often scandalized, thousands upon thousands of sinners were converted, often from the lowest socio-economic sectors of society - the very people Jesus had ministered to.

Then as today, the Salvationists waged a war on poverty and hunger wherever they were found. Like the apostles, it was not just evangelism they were interested in,- it was transformation of the whole person - spirit, soul and body. The Salvation Army became known around the world for its practical help of the poor and needy, just like the early church.

With their yellow, red and blue "BLOOD AND FIRE" flags, and their uniforms similar to the war uniforms of the day, these were God's spiritual assault commandos - fearless and radical evangelists for Jesus. It was not uncommon for them to pray all night (they called prayer "knee drill") and then preach all day. In 1883, the Salvation Army arrived in my home country of New Zealand. The "invading force" consisted of Lieutenant Edward Wright aged 19 years and Captain George Pollard aged 20 years. That was it. General Booth's resources were stretched thin by the enormous demand for Salvationist officers across the globe. Despite this, in a very short time the Army was headline news across New Zealand, and their street meetings were thronged with people. Within nine months it is reported that the fledgling Army in this country had 5000 converts. This scenario was repeated around the world.

In many respects, the Salvation Army was a young person's crusade. Many of the officers were very young, yet extremely zealous. In many ways this youth proved to be a great advantage rather than any kind of disadvantage.

In New Zealand, like England, Salvationists were arrested in significant numbers in the early days. In fact, as the court cases went on, these arrests ultimately caused such a public outcry that the New Zealand Parliament passed special legislation preventing the local City Councils from prosecuting the Salvation Army. Thus the imprisonments eventually died out.

However, the Salvationists also had enormous trouble in the early days from the "Skeleton Armies" and also the violent mobs that sometimes formed to break up their meetings. There were literally riots on the streets in England and around the world when the Salvation Army held their street-meetings and marches. At least one female officer in England was kicked to death by an angry mob, and many others were seriously injured. And amazingly it was not uncommon for the local Clergy to be involved in inciting these mobs. As often happens in Revivals, a large number of the church leaders of that time were bitterly opposed to this new move of God and its innovative and radical features. There was, perhaps, a certain amount of jealousy involved also. Certainly, many of them were motivated by a snobbish desire to keep the faith high and "pure", and not allow it to descend to the gutters of the street, where the Salvationists seemed to dwell. Raucous music and loud preaching on the streets, indeed! It apparently mattered little to them that many sinners were finding Jesus and that God was being glorified.

In 1912, the old warrior General William Booth passed on to glory. It was truly the end of an era - an era that had seen some of the most radical, anointed and effective Christianity in the history of the church. But like many movements after the original founders die, the Salvation Army then slowly began to settle down - to become respectable. And it gradually lost the innovation and the radical, fighting edge that had made it what it was. Actually, this is not unusual with Revival movements, though it is always sad to see it occur. The movements of Luther and Wesley, and even the early church all gradually went the same way after the founding fathers died. Today, we find a Salvation Army that is known more as a kindly and harmless social-welfare institution than a band of fearless warrior evangelists. The old uniforms are still there but the guerilla warfare is largely a thing of the remote past. The shell remains, but the 'heart' has slowly ebbed away.

But the vision, the passion and the zeal of the early Salvationists will never die completely. For the early histories are still just as much an inspiration today as they were when they were written.

And it is my belief that we are about to see a similar kind of street-movement arise in our day (because the times are just as desperate, if not more so, that they were then). And I believe that the early Salvation Army gives us significant pointers as to the character of this coming movement. The ministry of Jesus Himself was largely an open-air one, as was the 'early church' of the apostles (with thousands gathering daily in the open-air temple courtyard in Jerusalem, and the sick being healed on the streets). The great Awakening in Britain and America under Wesley and Whitefield was also a massive open-air movement. (In fact, Wesley was largely forced into open-air preaching when the pulpits of all England were closed to him). It was not uncommon for crowds of 20,000 to 30,000 people to gather in the open air to hear Wesley or Whitefield preach during this Revival. And it went on for many years.

It is interesting to note also that a new 'Revival music' arose with the Great Reformation under Martin Luther, as well as the Evangelical Awakening under Wesley 200 years later, and again with the Salvation Army Revivals a century after that. There was also a new 'Revival music' involved in the Welsh Revival of 1904, and to a degree, in other Revivals also. What I am trying to point out here is that if we are to see a new move of God's Spirit in our day (which I believe to be essential), particularly if it is to be a 'street-based' movement (I cannot see it any other way), then we should expect to see a new Revival STREET-MUSIC arise with it.

We live in a society today in which the church has been losing ground and losing influence massively over a thirty-year period. Every year, the number of youth suicides climbs, the programs on television grow ever-sicker, and people's open contempt for our tepid Christianity increases. These facts alone (even without all the other damning statistics) are enough to show just how little we are positively impacting our world today. The brutal fact is that in our present state, we are far too tame, too safe, too insipid and too predictable to ever do any serious damage to the devil. And he is clearly beating us hands down. If we were damaging him seriously, he would raise up violent persecution against us. But he simply doesn't need to bother these days. Better to let us sleep. The most staggering fact of all is that when people enter our churches, we can often be found singing little self-congratulatory songs about how "victorious" and 'mighty' we are. And there is no end of talk about the 'blessings' that God is showering upon us. COME ON, CHURCH! GET REAL! TELL ME, WHERE IS THIS 'VICTORY' YOU SPEAK OF?

There is one interesting facet to the Laodicean church which often goes unremarked. Jesus described this 'lukewarm' church as being "wretched, and miserable, and poor, and BLIND, and naked" (even though they thought of themselves as spiritually 'rich' and in need of nothing). The thing I want to point to, is that Jesus described the Laodicean church as "blind" - blind to their own state and blind to how far below God's standards they had fallen. They couldn't see it at all. Today's church is like this. We exist in a state of warm and comfortable compromise. But you would never know it from the way we talk. We talk like militant generals and act like spiritual wimps. As I said before, this all has to change, and it has to change FAST. For we are losing a generation.

Compared to even the committed Christians of the West today, William Booth and his early Salvationists were outrageous zealots. So were Luther, Wesley, Whitefield and their followers. The plain fact is, we are far too "nice" to the devil today. We are giving him an easy ride. Tell me, is God ever going to find warriors in our day such as those who fought for Him in ages past? Where on earth will He find such 'men and women of valor'? As the Bible says, "the eyes of the Lord run to and fro throughout the whole earth, to show Himself strong in the behalf of them whose heart is perfect toward Him" (2 Chron 16:9). Tell me, friend, will you be one who will heed His call?

I am convinced that God is about to take drastic action, as He has done in similar situations right down through history, whether the church is ready for it or not. I believe that we are once again about to see a "street-church" birthed in Revival power, to route the enemy and to rouse all who are 'at ease in Zion'. The Bible is very clear that God cannot live with an insipid, Laodicean church. He has taken drastic measures before, and He will do so again. I do not believe He can afford to have a compromised Christianity being walked all over by the devil day-in and day-out. Surely He is again about to raise up an army who will do battle with the devil for this generation, and who will not lie down until true victory is gained. I am convinced that God is looking for soldiers today - true commandos who will literally "love not their lives unto the death" - men and women who truly possess the heart of Isaiah: "I heard the voice of the Lord, saying, Whom shall I send, and who will go for us? Then said I, HERE AM I; SEND ME" (Isa 6:8).

As outlined in the Introduction to this book, in the early 1990's my wife and I began our compromising alternative band, which God in His mercy only allowed us to continue for a relatively short time. We had been involved in various bands before this, also. Ironically, it had essentially been the whole "early Salvation Army" thing that had inspired me to get involved in music in the first place. In my late teens I had begun to read up on the early Salvationists and what they had done. I believed strongly (and still do) that it was God who inspired me to read and become fired-up by their example. So our first band was a street band. We had a portable sound system, portable drums and amplifiers, etc. But the main thing that we obviously lacked was the Revival anointing and godly power of the early Salvationists. After awhile, I began to drift away from this vision, and we became more 'professional', starting to become just like any conventional band. And the temptation to compromise so as to give ourselves a better chance of "making it" began to have more of an appeal.

As I have said, God eventually pulled the plug on our compromised alternative band in no uncertain terms. And as soon as I made this decision, I came back into a very close relationship with God again, possibly even stronger than when I was first filled with the Holy Spirit some years before. All I wanted to do was to commune with Him. The band had obviously become an "idol" that had been partially blocking my relationship with the Father. (And many ministries today are the same. Too busy "building" to walk closely with God - A proven recipe for disaster). Brothers, sisters, we have to have our priorities right. If our 'ministry' takes us away from walking and communing intimately with God as Adam used to do, in the "cool of the day", then we had better reassess everything. Is this God's kingdom you are building, or is it your own?

After the shock of finding out the truth about our band, I just wanted to forget about music. I had been involved in video production, band management and recording also, but now I wanted nothing more to do with any of it. And so we sold as much of our gear as we could. But funnily enough, the vision for a "street-Revival", a radical street-music and an army of God that would shake the world (similar to the early Salvation Army) never completely died in me. In fact, it kept burning away, deep inside me, and I couldn't shake it off.

It was some months later that we received some amazing confirmation out of the blue, from a source that we had never come across before. This came in the form of a taped message by American preacher James Ryle, who had been given a series of dreams and visions several years earlier which spoke at length of the new "street-music" that would arise with the coming Revival. Now I was not terribly into this area of 'dreams and visions' at that time (though I knew they were found throughout the Bible), but almost everything James Ryle said on those tapes just resonated so strongly with what God had shown me – it was uncanny. My wife was really surprised. And the anointing of God was so strong in places when I was listening, that I just literally wept. Below is a recent synopsis of these dreams by James Ryle. I hope that as you read them you will see why they affected me the way they did, and I also hope that those of you who are musicians will be inspired and blessed by them as much as I was:

The Sons of Thunder - A synopsis of Dreams
by James Ryle.

"The following insight occurred to me in August 1990 as a result of three dreams. In the first dream I saw a flatbed trailer with a curtain behind it. This trailer was parked at a fairground, as if a concert was about to happen. There were two guitars on the mobile stage. The color of these guitars was the most vivid, electric blue that one could imagine. What impressed me most was that the guitars were not painted, but stained. It had obviously taken time to make them blue. The curtain was the same color as the guitars. Two men walked from behind the curtain with sheet music in their hands. They were very excited, and could hardly wait to play this music. One said to the other, "Wait till they hear this. Its going to be just like when the Beatles played their music!" In the dream I also became excited. I turned to see the crowd that was gathering at the stage and the scene changed before my eyes. The audience became a vast body of water, like a lake, and as the musicians played the new song I saw fishing lines cast out into the water. The dream ended. My waking thoughts were that God is about to release a new kind of song in the streets. It will bring a revelation of the truth and it will usher people into His presence. The anointing of the Lord will be with musicians who have spent time in God's presence "behind the curtain" receiving a deep love for the lost. The lyrics of their songs will be as "fishing lines" cast into the hearts of men and women needing Christ.

In the second dream, I was on the stage in a large church. There was an equipment room on the right side of the stage. It had microphones, cables, amplifiers and other kinds of things that collect in closets. In one corner of the room I saw a power amplifier covered with dust. The cord was wrapped about it, and it had not been used for a long time. When I looked closer I saw written on the front, "The Beatles Power Amp." I knew in that moment that this box was the source of their sound and their power. I knew that anyone could plug into this box and, in effect, have what the Beatles had - an incredible ability to mobilize masses of people to a single thing. As I stood there holding the

Beatles power amplifier, I asked aloud this question, "What is this doing here in the Church's equipment room?" Suddenly I was out of the equipment room and standing behind the pulpit at this church, still holding the amp. The enormous church, throughout the main floor and all about the balcony, was packed with people from every nation. A very beautiful woman, radiant with a glow of glory, stood in the middle of the church and began singing a song from the Lord. A light shone upon her and her voice filled the auditorium. All she sang was: "In the name of Jesus Christ the Lord we say unto you, be saved." She sang it over and over. She would turn to her right and sing, then turn to her left and sing; then she would turn behind her and before her and sing the same thing. As I watched her sing, it was like a wind blowing on a wheat field. The people began to swoon in the presence of God and then collapse in their seats -- converted to Christ! God's power was moving through the music. The dream ended.

My thoughts upon waking were clear. There is going to be a new sound and distinctive anointing from the Lord upon music that will turn the heads and capture the hearts of men and women for Jesus. The reason the Beatles power Amp was in the Church's equipment room is because God meant for it to be a part of the church's equipment in reaching the lost for Christ. Music does not belong to the world, but to the Church. Music does not belong to the Devil, but to Christ. Satan has indeed stolen the hearts of musicians and their gift of music to use for his own evil purposes. The Church in many cases has unwittingly surrendered this to the devil without any fight at all. Music was given to worship the Lord but Satan has turned it for self-worship, which is the reason people tend to worship musicians. But true worship and true music belong to Jesus Christ. They are given to His church to serve Him with. I truly believe the anointing the Lord will release on music is going to sweep the world in a manner like the Beatles did when they first performed. But instead of drawing attention to themselves (like the Beatles did), the anointed musicians of the Lord will draw attention to Christ alone and give Him all the glory.

In the third dream I was again in the large church where I had seen the amplifier. This time the church was empty except for one man. He was up on stage playing a keyboard and singing to the Lord. It was a beautiful song, and he was crying because of the tender exchange taking place between he and Jesus. He was writing the song right there, spontaneously making it up as he went. I was greatly moved by this song and the man's pure worship. I had a camera with me and decided to take a picture of this to remember it. I took two Polaroid pictures that came out immediately. When I looked at these pictures I was stunned because both of them were glowing with a golden light. I looked up and then I could see it on the man. The entire platform around him was also glowing like gold. I knew that this was the anointing of God. I showed the man, but it startled him...He looked at the pictures for a second, putting his hands in his pockets he shrugged his shoulders and kicked the ground shyly. "Gosh, I didn't know you were here, I'm so embarrassed" was all he could say. "You don't have to apologize for the anointing" I replied. The dream changed. I still had the two photographs of the anointed worshipper in one hand, and in the other I held a parchment. I looked at the scroll and saw it was a letter written by an unknown soldier in the Salvation Army. It said, "The Lord will release into the streets an army of worshipping warriors known as the Sons of Thunder. They will bring forth a witness of worship and praise for the Lord Jesus Christ that will bring many people to God."

The dream changed once more. I was floating over a wide and long highway that headed in one direction. All lanes were completely grid-locked, jam packed with motorcycle gang members, revving their engines and stirring up dust. It was a graphic picture of lost humanity. Then I saw a group of bikers moving in single file along the service road. They were headed for a field in the distance where there was a monolithic stone. This stone, I knew in the dream, represented the power of Christ and would empower those who touched it to go back to the highway and turn masses of lost people back to God. I looked closer at these motorcyclists as they sped toward the Stone, and saw on their jackets the words "Sons of Thunder."

As the Sons of Thunder approached the Stone to touch it, a barricade of law officers stood arm to arm in riot gear, opposing the motorcyclists - assuming they were intent on defacing the Stone.

At that moment, I took the parchment in my hand and folded it like a paper airplane. I then placed the photographs inside it and tossed it to sail over the heads of the officers. I knew that if the pictures and the promise were to touch the Stone, then the power would be released upon the Sons of Thunder. When the paper was one foot away from the monument, just before actually touching the Stone, my dream ended. I believe this portrays the role of intercessory prayer in helping the Church get past the barricades of legalism, and open the gifts of God for reaching the lost with the message of Christ. The Sons of Thunder, represented by motorcyclists on the service road, illustrate the servant heart of ministry. They also show the agility and decisiveness necessary in reaching the lost. The fact that they were in single file shows, in my opinion, the unity we must maintain as Christians in order for our message about Christ to have credibility...

Now, I extend to you a prayer that God will capture your heart and bring you into full devotion to Christ Jesus. That your passion for music will be equaled by your love for the lost. I pray that you will receive an anointing from God to minister with artistic creativity that is so compelling in its quality, and in its message - that thousands of unbelievers who are lost in darkness will see the light and turn to Jesus to be cleansed and born again!"

One of the parts that touched me most in the above dreams was the part where James was given a parchment written by an unknown soldier of the early Salvation Army. It said, "The Lord will release into the streets an army of worshipping warriors known as the Sons of Thunder. They will bring forth a witness of worship and praise for the Lord Jesus Christ that will bring many people to God." I doubt whether I could sum up my own vision for the coming street-Revival any better. And I have since found that God has been speaking to many, many praying people right around the world about this street-church. How desperately such a movement is needed today! God has got to have an army in this generation who will pray and fight and win, even under the most trying of circumstances. And whether today's church would understand such an army or not, I believe that it is very much on the way. In fact, I am convinced that this movement is now truly imminent.

For many years now, there have been prophecies around the world that God is about to visit tremendous "shaking" upon the church. We have already seen that today's Christianity is far from ideal - even far from adequate. And today's world is a godless wasteland - without hope or meaning - for many of our youth. It is at times exactly like these that God has chosen to move in the past. But such moves are often far from "comfortable" for the church. And it is clear that what God has been speaking about lately is a coming 'REFORMATION', not merely a Revival. As the Bible tells us, Judgment begins "at the house of God" (1 Pet 4:17). He will always set His own house in order before starting on the world. But such Reformations (and their leaders) are often made most unwelcome by the church. For they are never "quiet, retiring" men or movements, and everything they stand for often amounts to one giant rebuke for the church. Was Luther welcomed, or Wesley, or Booth? Hardly! In fact, they were some of the most controversial figures of their day. Like Israel with her prophets, the church has rarely greeted Reformers or Revivalists with open arms. In fact, quite the reverse. It has often been the church leaders who have persecuted new moves of God the worst.

It is very clear that when we speak of a "street-Revival", we are not just talking about an army of godly street-warriors or of the 'new music' that will accompany them. The coming Reformation must obviously go much deeper than this. For the whole church is in a sickly and tepid state. I believe that what is coming will bring great shaking and transformation to the whole of the system and structure of the Western church, not to mention the Christians themselves. For this is exactly the kind of clean-out that is so desperately needed. And God has never shrunk back from sending in His "specialists" and taking such drastic action before, when it has been necessary.

In his synopsis, James Ryle mentions the UNITY that must prevail amongst Christians in order for our message to have credibility. This is absolutely right. But it is hardly the picture that we present to outsiders today. In fact, to all appearances, today's Christian church is hopelessly divided, with it's dozens of competing denominations and fellowships. As a Generation X-er myself, I would have to say that this is one of the most significant factors holding back today's young people from responding to our message. They see all the competing little religious groups, each off in its own corner building its own little kingdom, and they say to themselves, "Where is God in all of this?" And they are quite right to ask. For Christianity was never like this in the beginning. Jesus Himself prayed: "That they all may be ONE... that the world may BELIEVE" (Jn 17:21). And the book of Acts records that: "the multitude of them that believed were all of one heart and one soul" (Acts 4:32). There were no denominations in the early church.

At the moment, we have evangelical, Spirit-filled Christians living on the same street who hardly know each other. We all go off to our separate little fellowships each Sunday, and attend our own church's little home-groups, etc. Thus Christians who basically believe the same things are utterly (and permanently) divided. We have created a "system" of separate fellowships that divides the church. And our leadership system just perpetuates it all. (For that is what they are taught to do. It is their career that is supported by this system, after all).

Just imagine that some miracle occurred, and all the church buildings closed down so that all the Christians in a town simply met together in a local park. Preaching, worship, healing, etc - out in the open air. ALMOST EVERY DAY. And true UNITY for once. None of these little private kingdoms. And imagine if, instead of going to meetings just with people from "your fellowship", you gathered in homes with the LOCAL Christians from your street. The Lord's Supper, baptisms and spiritual gifts such as tongues, interpretation, prophecy, spiritual songs and teaching occurring in Christians' homes all the time (1 Cor 14:26). And no "labels" or denominations in sight. Just the LOCAL church in someone's home. What a powerful thing this would be! Now what I am describing here is EXACTLY WHAT THE EARLY CHURCH WAS LIKE. Large open-air gatherings and small local home-fellowships. It's not too complicated, is it? In fact, it is very simple. There is almost nothing stopping us from adopting this powerful, unified model of Church Life right away, if we wished. So why don't we just do it? I'll tell you why. Because we have built a "system" based on division and we don't want to step outside it (no matter how foolish or destructive it is). We are comfortable with the status quo, and we don't want to risk such a radical change. (Too many vested interests also - let's face it).

But do you think these excuses sound reasonable to God? I think not. If there is no good reason not to have a "street-church" like the book of Acts, then it is my belief that God will bring about such a 'shaking' that we will be FORCED to adopt such a model. For this is what God has been speaking about everywhere - a 'church without walls'. True unity, just like the early church. And there is no reason why we could not do it right now. It is only our "systems" and structures that are holding us back. Instead of them serving us, we have ended up serving them. And we have lost a tremendous amount of credibility with the world because of it. Imagine what a powerful testimony such unity would be!

I am convinced that the above is no pie-in-the-sky dream. It is the reality that God desires so desperately. This is all very much part of the STREET-CHURCH that we have been talking about. And if God has to SHAKE THE CHURCH STRUCTURE TO PIECES in order to bring this about, then I am convinced that He will. (He has done this before. And desperate times really do call for desperate measures). We are about to enter a period of great Reformation in the church. This is what God has been telling praying people right around the world. I honestly believe that He would be able to use and bless the church enormously if we just sorted out some of these basic problems. Even without a great outpouring of God's Spirit, I believe that such changes IN THEMSELVES would bring about tremendous harvest and blessing. May He open the eyes of every one of us to these possibilities. A lot of us are simply thinking TOO SMALL.

Chapter Nine

DEFEATING GOLIATH

There is no doubt that tremendous courage and DARING will be required by those who are seeking to become part of this 'street-Revival' that we have been talking about. For today's church is now so far behind the eight-ball, that these street-warriors will be faced with a monumental task. This is why I believe God is willing to take such drastic measures. And this is also why I believe He is looking for BOLD and RADICAL men and women to use in this Revival.

I recently had the opportunity to watch the movie "Braveheart" on video (I had seen it before), and I found myself greatly affected by the spiritual parallels I saw in this stunning film. Whether the rendering of William Wallace's life in the movie is accurate or not, I found it an inspiration to uncompromising courage, daring, resourcefulness and valor. The film has a majesty about it which transcends much of Hollywood's usual "product".

In 'Braveheart', the people of Scotland were a vanquished and defeated race, their hopes and dreams for their nation in ruins. They were kept firmly under the thumb of a harsh, foreign king, and their nobles had compromised and kowtowed to this ruler in order to keep the peace. But eventually, when the people could take almost no more humiliation, an aggressive young man arose - though not of noble parentage - to lead the warriors of Scotland into battle and victory. And for a time their nation was free once more. (These victories were built upon to great effect by Robert the Bruce several years later). Scotland was once again free from tyrannical rule.

But the thing that struck me most about this film, was that the majestically daring spirit displayed by William Wallace throughout it was exactly the kind of DARING TENACITY that I believe God requires of all who wish to be part of the coming move of God. After having studied many of the great Reformers and Revivalists of past ages, I believe God spoke to me several years ago about the major qualification required to enter into the coming Reformation / Revival. He simply told me: "WHO DARES WINS". For whoever takes part in what is coming must fight and win against tremendous odds.

If there is one spirit which imbues the film 'Braveheart', it is this spirit of DARING. And likewise, a Scripture which I have often been reminded of is: "From the days of John the Baptist until now, the kingdom of heaven suffers violence, and the violent take it by force" (Mt 11:12). It is clearly not enough to preach (though preaching is good). And it is clearly not enough even to pray (though praying is good also). For as always, only those who DARE will win their way through into the coming move of God . Ours is to be a 'violent' faith - a 'violent' DARING, which takes the kingdom by force. Only then will true Revival and Reformation come down.

In Martin Luther's day, many leaders were well aware that some form of Reformation was essential. But they were shocked at the daring of Luther, who took on the whole Roman Catholic empire and won. For there is a day for RECKLESS DARING, and my friends, THAT DAY IS NOW. We are told in the book of Revelation what the attributes that defeat the devil are: "And they overcame him by the blood of the Lamb, and by the word of their testimony; AND THEY LOVED NOT THEIR LIVES UNTO THE DEATH" (Rev 12:11).

It is noticeable at such times that there are many "prudent" souls who counsel caution and 'gradualism'. (In the movie, it was the compromising Scottish nobles). And so it will be today also. But I am convinced that the day for such lukewarm "prudence" is now over. Things are far worse than a lot of Christians realize. It's just that we have grown used to it. We have been immersed in it for so long that we have become acclimatized to a situation in which the devil is stomping all over the church. We have come to accept this as "normal". Friends, I am convinced that the days of timidity and hiding our lamp under a bushel are now gone. Surely the time has come to beat our plowshares into swords and our pruning hooks into spears, to shout alarm from the housetops, and to gird ourselves for war.

I am so desperately tired of today's tepid, ineffectual Christianity. Surely the day for 'violent' action has come? I am a great admirer of David, who when he saw Goliath mouthing threats and insults against the people of God, said: " Who is this uncircumcised Philistine, that he should defy the armies of the living God?" Did he stop to take "counsel" from his 'prudent' advisers? No! Did he stop even to hold a series of prayer meetings about the situation? No! The honour of His God was at stake, and HE WAS READY TO TAKE ON THE ENEMY IN HIS NAME. The other thing I like about David was that he RAN out to meet Goliath. Now this was a violent, daring faith in action. Tell me friend, are you ready to run out to meet the enemies of God?

The Scripture tells us that when the army of Gideon was being chosen, the first ones that were eliminated were the "fearful and afraid". And then God cut the army right down to 300 men through other means. You see, God likes it when the odds against victory are huge, because then men will not take the credit when victory is achieved. It is God who will get the glory. And those 300 utterly routed all the thousands of the combined armies of the Midianites and the Amalekites who filled the valley "like grasshoppers for multitude" (Judg 7:12). I tell you, such days come again. Friend, might you be a part of God's army who will win through to victory in these dark days?

It is my belief that God is looking for men and women today who are willing to pay the price for all-out war with the devil, and even to suffer rejection from their Christian brothers at times as well. For such has often been the case with true Revival. War is never comfortable. War is never easy or "nice". True war involves daring and confrontation, guts and aggression. And I believe that the eyes of the Lord are roving the earth in our day, seeking those who truly possess this DARING FAITH, to draft them into His army, to do battle on His behalf. The storm clouds darken our horizon today, the sounds of battle can be heard in the far distance, and the days of all-out warfare come - in fact they are at our door.

Friends, if you do not possess the DARING that God has said is the minimum requirement to partake in this battle, then all I can advise you is: GET SOME NOW. (Perhaps watching 'Braveheart' might be a good place to start?)

Chapter Ten

CLOSING THOUGHTS

We have seen in previous chapters how the situations in both the church and the world today make Revival utterly essential. Things simply cannot go on the way they are. And it is my belief that God is going to greatly use technology and the media in any coming move of His Spirit. Just as Luther's Reformation and other great movements were greatly furthered by the invention of the printing press and other media technologies down through the ages, so I believe that the scores of millions in the West today can only be reached if we allow God to use today's modern technologies. The Internet, email, MP3s, DVDs, videos, computers, and even secular radio and television - these and other means will all be used by God in a new and very anointed way, I believe. But they must be secured and used only under God's direction, and they must not compromise the original gospel in any sense.

A number of commentators have noted that Generations X and Y are particularly enamored with modern technology. This is true, but remember, the youth of today have grown up in a culture that has been utterly immersed in electronic media for decades. What we are dealing with here is the first total TV generation. And there are some real problems that come with this.

As the brilliant writer Neil Postman points out, enormous changes have come about just through TELEVISION being our dominant world medium today. For television BY IT'S VERY NATURE trivializes almost everything it touches (often reducing it to a few 'sound-bites'), thus altering its content and almost everything else about it. And being the dominant medium, all the other media scramble to become more and more like television.

TV is overwhelmingly an 'ENTERTAINMENT' medium, made up of fast-flowing images designed to capture our attention and keep it. It is a medium largely ruled by ratings and the advertising dollar. And the problem is, that because television is the most powerful and dominant form of communication in our world today, every other form of communication tends to conform to its ways and its appeal. You see this with politics. It doesn't matter so much how honest or how efficient a politician is these days. What matters most is how well they come across on TV. Do they look presentable (or better still, photogenic) in front of the cameras, and can they speak in newsworthy sound-bites to fit the TV news? These are the factors that will get a politician into high office today. (Sad really, isn't it?)

As I said, television is the dominant form of communication in our age, and every other medium must either conform or die. This even applies to communicators such as school-teachers and preachers. Last century, when literature and oratory were the world's dominant media, it was not uncommon for preachers to speak for one or two hours at a time. And the same was true of politicians. But today people will not stand for this, because they have become conditioned by the media to have shorter and shorter attention spans. Speak to any schoolteacher today and you will hear what a battle it is for them to keep the kids' attention, when what they are really doing is competing with the pace and interest-value of television. The kids are used to multi-colored entertainment-fests and 30-second whizz-bang commercials delivered to their living room through a little box in the corner. I ask you: How is a teacher supposed to compete with that? (It's no good putting all our education onto TV. For television is a trance-like medium, with very little interactive value - not great for education). Thus, teachers are essentially forced to speak in 'sound-bites' and keep everything as colorful, fast-paced and entertaining as they can in order to compete. Can you see how the dominance of television is bringing about conformity in all the other forms of communication as well? Even magazines have to become more visually stimulating, colorful and superficial in order to compete.

And it is not only the format, but also the CONTENT of the message that is affected by television. For certain things like color, excitement, action, brevity and shallowness work well on TV, but things like deep discussion, lengthy debate and real (not shallow) investigation usually come across poorly. It is very much a medium made for sensationalism, cheap thrills and entertainment, though it often pretends to have genuine depth. A good example of this is what happens with 'news' on TV. Have you ever noticed that it is the stories with the good pictures, the pithy sound-bites or the 'shock-horror' angles that end up on the TV news? These items are presented in grave tones as though they are the most momentous news stories of the day. But if it is just 'talking heads', forget it. People want to see action. So the skydiver who went out of control somewhere (caught on video!) or the bizarre disaster in some unheard-of place (great pictures!) will make the TV news, while the more important (but dull) story may be shoved aside.

The same is true of 'documentaries'. Most of them (and the TV news in general) should be openly acknowledged as 'info-tainment' rather than real news. They choose subjects that they know will push people's buttons, or that have that vital 'human-interest' angle. And in most news programs, there is only the briefest of moments to explore some of the most complicated issues. Thus the tendency to sensationalize, trivialize or distort issues so that they can be reported in 30 seconds flat.

And as you can imagine, such distortion will radically affect any attempt at televising the gospel unless we are very careful. For as an advertising and entertainment medium, television brings an overwhelming temptation to make our gospel 'entertaining', positive and un-threatening when we appear on the screen. (As the old advertising saying goes, "Eliminate the negative and accentuate the positive"). We must be very aware of these subtle pressures to conform.

There can be no doubt that the dominance of television has had an enormous role in many of the problems that we have discussed in this book. For example, the shallowness and 'entertainment-value' of our gospel today has without doubt been greatly influenced by the dominance of this medium. (In the same way as school-teaching has). Preachers have felt the need to 'compete' with the shallow gloss of TV hype. Thus we have a glossy gospel that promises all kinds of wonderful things (though not the taking up of the cross) if only we will "come to Jesus". And it is clear also, that television has greatly added to the appeal of hedonism (the pursuit of pleasure as an over-riding goal) and materialism (the pursuit of possessions) and has also greatly contributed to the general depravity and sickness infecting the West today. Every year, television seems to lead us further down the road to Gomorrah.

Having said all of this, however, it is important to note that most of today's youth have been fed to the back teeth with entertainment and hype, to the point where it no longer has as much of an allure for them. In fact, Generations X and Y are notoriously cynical and unresponsive toward hype of any kind. (Which is why we have a rash of anti-hype commercials and anti-hero films at the moment). They can see through it almost straight away. This is one gigantic reason that, instead of trying to "entertain" the youth into the kingdom, we should be issuing a massive CHALLENGE to them instead. Entertainment, gloss and hype are losing their luster, but thus far there is no real alternative as far as most young people can see, so they just keep on pursuing shallow escapism. But many of them are becoming pretty bored with it all. I tell you, the group or the movement that will be DARING ENOUGH to give these young people a cause worth dying for, rather than trying to entertain them, will take the unassailable high ground and will win this generation.

Most Gen X-ers understand TV, its dominance, and the environment it has created instinctively. For they have grown up in this era. The electronic media are like water and air to them - an integral part of their daily lives. I believe that this is a tremendous advantage for Christians from this generation who want to break through the 'entertainment' conventions of the worldwide media today, and use them for God instead. For you have to know the rules in order to break them. I am convinced that we do not have to abide by all the old conventions that govern television and the other media today. The new generation is fast tiring of them anyway. They are almost 'entertained to death' in today's world. So I believe it is now possible to turn some of these entertainment conventions on their head. But only if we are very bold. Those who understand television instinctively will know which conventions can be broken and which can't. What I am saying is that the world's media (including TV) is now wide open for change, because their AUDIENCE is wide open for change. I tell you, revolution is in the air once more. But who will launch most effectively at the starting gun? Will it be the devil or will it be us?

Probably the only thing that comes close to television in terms of influence amongst today's youth is MUSIC. In fact, at its best, music is quite capable of leading the way and dominating all the other media, which I am sure you will agree is an incredible feat. This was certainly the case in the 1960's, when the Beatles utterly dominated every other art or communications medium as far as influence went. However, television has become far more sophisticated since then. But I still believe that music is capable of dominating today's media and communications landscape in a profound way, just as it did in the sixties. The only reason this is not happening now is that the world has not seen another group quite like the Beatles since their demise. (In fact, in many ways, no group has even come close. How many bands do you know that have had the top five single chart positions in America ALL AT THE SAME TIME?)

I was very intrigued by the dreams that were given to James Ryle in which he saw a gifting and ability like that of the Beatles being made available to the church. I have to say that this touched a chord with me, because I am convinced that in order for there to be a spiritual 'revolution' in the West sufficient to turn the youth back to God en masse, there has to be something that will dominate the 'voice' of the media. And God-inspired, Spirit-fired music clearly has the potential to do just that.

How desperately such a movement is needed in our day. But as James Ryle stated in his synopsis, the most important activity in seeing this vision come to pass is intercession. Prayer, as always, is the key.

It is clear that largely, all the devil has to do to dominate the West is to dominate our media. And this is obviously exactly what he does. Over time, he can greatly influence the thinking, beliefs and expectations of millions of people with subtle media propaganda. No wonder he is called the "prince of the power of the air" (Eph 2:2). Ever since the Garden of Eden, he has specialized in selling cleverly-packaged lies and deception to human beings. This is how he dominates our world. So it is little wonder that when we go behind the scenes in large media organizations we often find some rather disturbing people in key positions. Almost as if they had been hand-picked for the job. But even people such as these will be simply unable to hold back the huge tidal wave of media-Revival that is coming. And we will take back the high ground over our cities once again.

Some people may well be asking at this point whether Christians shouldn't be throwing out their TV sets and boycotting the media, because of the sickness that is propagated throughout our society. I can quite understand this. Our own family does not even have a television – and our children don't suffer for it at all. In fact, quite the opposite! But we do have DVD players, which allows us to really "choose" what is being watched - and monitor its influence in our home.

Numerous studies have shown that television in itself is actually very bad for children's development and general well-being. While they are in this trance-like state, children are missing out on developing skills such as reading, use of their imagination, physical fitness and hand-eye coordination, etc. None of this is good for them. But I can't imagine starting a 'crusade' to rid the world of television. I think we have to face the fact that this medium is dominant in the communications culture of our age, and know how to work around and within that situation. This is not impossible, and in fact I am convinced that news and footage of the coming Revival will be carried around the world by such media.

And for similar reasons I am not enormously upset that there has been such an inter-marriage between the secular and the Christian music companies. We have already looked at the harm that this has done, but I am also convinced that this situation has the potential for much good. For if God can find Christian artists today who will not give way to idolatry, pride, showmanship or compromise, I am convinced that it is possible for openly Christian music (the 'Sons of Thunder'?) to make it onto the secular airwaves. The industry is now set up in such a way as to make this very possible.

I see as reality a coming move of God where the secular music charts will be full of Christian music, the Music Video stations will be full of Christian songs and interviews, and the TV news will be full of footage of a great street-Revival, with thousands of young people gathered on the streets in Jesus' name. I do not believe that this is a mere pipe-dream. In fact, I consider such a movement to be imperative if we are ever going to claim back this generation for God. God has done this kind of thing before, and I am convinced, from what He has been saying right around the world, that He is about to do so again. None of this is impossible. But obviously, it would take a series of tremendous miracles for the devil to be defeated on such a scale. And God clearly specializes in such miracles. But do we dare believe in Him to accomplish such a thing? And will we heed His call to become radical enough in our Christianity to be part of such a thing?

I truly believe that we will one day see thousands of young people gathered in the open air, praising and glorifying God. The sick will be healed, the gospel will be preached, and God will be magnified for all to see. This is what the church was always meant to be like. I believe that God is calling us to stop hiding our lamp under a bushel - to stop hiding away in our little buildings and organizations - and to get out there and BE THE CHURCH, out on the streets where we are meant to be. Glory to God!

At this point, I would just like to briefly discuss some of the practical aspects of being involved in music ministry today. I have had to ponder some of these issues long and hard, because we have had to deal with them on a practical level with our own music over the years.

It seems clear that the most important qualifications for becoming involved in music ministry are SPIRITUAL ones. For it matters little to God how wonderful a musician we are, if we do not have a close and deep walk with Him. God desperately desires HUMBLE servants in music ministry today who delight in GLORIFYING HIM and who do not secretly crave the limelight or the praises of men for themselves. It is so easy to lose sight of these fundamental things in music ministry these days. The temptation to soak up the applause and to show off one's talents has destroyed the spiritual depth of many music ministers. Music is a field that tends overwhelmingly toward idolatry, and if we are not watchful, this industry is quite capable of devouring us and our spirituality whole. What God is looking for today is not slick showmanship, but rather a deep and enduring love towards Him - a love that is built upon such a firm foundation that nothing can quench or smother it. And if God has to take many years building this into us, then He will do exactly that before releasing us into our ministry. Deep and lengthy preparation in the 'wilderness' was the key to the success of many ministries in the Bible, and the same should be true today. Our relationship with God must be truly built upon a Rock in order to survive.

We have already discussed one of the most basic issues faced by music ministries today - that of charging money at the door for people to hear us play. As I said earlier in this book, I simply cannot go along with this practice at all. But what if we are invited to play at a large festival, where the people have already been charged money to get in? Well, obviously, if God wants us to minister at such an event, then by all means we should go. But I believe that if it is up to us (i.e., if it is one of our own concerts), then we should not charge people admission.

I must say that my thinking on this and many other issues has been helped enormously by reading the Biography of Keith Green entitled 'No Compromise'. I would certainly recommend this book to any young musicians today (in fact, to anyone).

Another issue that Keith Green himself faced was whether or not it is even reasonable for Christians to charge money for the sale of their records. Keith's own conclusion, reached after much anguish, was to offer the records at the standard price through the shops, but to have copies available for those who could not afford them, for whatever donation they could make. This is quite a fraught issue, as people are actually paying to buy a physical object which has cost quite a large sum to produce and distribute. It is a bit different from just simple ministry (for which we should never charge). I admire what Keith did, and feel that we should probably all attempt to have a similar policy in place. But like Keith, I believe that if we want to get our music out to the world, then there is almost no hope of doing so effectively unless we basically use the standard channels. It just becomes an impractical and virtually impossible task otherwise. (Go through the whole exercise of everything that happens to an album - from recording to distribution to sale - and multiply that by tens of thousands of copies - and you will see what I mean. We just can't afford to waste our time doing all of this ourselves. Let the existing "machine" do its job!)

However, one thing I do believe is that the new music ministries should avoid signing directly to any existing Record Company. What we should be doing is setting up independent labels and then "licensing" our albums to the larger Companies to market and distribute (though we should insist on having some say over the marketing). This is not uncommon practice in today's industry. I also believe that such labels should basically be charitable institutions - using their profits to help the poor.

Above all things, I believe that music ministry (and particularly live performance) should be extremely HONEST in every sense.

Like true preaching, we must be transparent before God and before the people. This is not to be some 'show' or stage-act, nor merely some contrived attempt to manipulate peoples' emotions. Our songs must be straight from the heart - expressing our deepest feelings, longings and heart-attitudes. For example, it is clearly no good writing songs about 'war' if we are not naturally war-like in our attitude to the devil's works. If we are only TRYING to be war-like, then the songs just won't come across as real or honest. And for the same reason, it is no good singing worship songs to God if our over-riding desire is not to utterly glorify Him. What a disaster if the deep motive of our heart is really to glorify ourselves or to show off our own talents.

I am convinced that, like the early Salvation Army, the music of God's new army must contain the war-like aggression and the heart-felt worship that lies at the very heart of all they stand for. The music they produce will represent who they really are. This must be a true Revival movement, producing a gritty (and often quite simple) yet anointed Revival music. Wouldn't it be wonderful to literally capture the "sound of heaven" and bring it down to earth? What a 'pure' form of music! How simple yet how glorious. Both worship and warfare together. Is it not possible that this is exactly what God desires - for His true musicians to capture the sound of heaven and bring it down amongst men?

ZEAL FOR THE KINGDOM

I believe it is time again for a new zeal to arise in the church in our day. I can no longer believe in a Christianity that every day loses more and more ground to the devil. I cannot believe in a church that will not FIGHT for every inch of territory that the devil calls his own. And I cannot go along with a Christianity that lolls in comfort while a lost world gropes blindly on in darkness and sin. Like Nero who played his fiddle while Rome burned, we sit back in our cozy little boxes and allow the storms to ravage the poor, the needy and the desperate. But will not the Judge of all the earth do right? I am afraid I cannot believe in a structure and a system that has become a ball and chain around our collective necks.

I am convinced that the time has now come for us to break out of our chains of conformity, comfort and compromise. It is time to hit the devil hard, and to keep on hitting him with wave after wave of untrammeled aggression. We have been too "nice" for far too long. God needs holy warriors today, who will give no quarter in a war to the death if need be. As the Bible states, we "have not yet resisted unto blood, striving against sin" (Heb 12:4).

The great tragedy of this hour is that GOD IS NOT GLORIFIED in the earth. We are failing dismally to display His glory to a dying world. And thus the world cannot know Him. Indeed, in many cases we hardly know Him ourselves. There is actually only one word - the word "HOLY" - that is used three times in a row (for maximum emphasis) in the whole of Scripture: "Holy, holy, holy, Lord God Almighty..." (Rev 4:8). Thus it must be taken that God's HOLINESS is the attribute which perhaps comes closest to representing the very core of His being and His character. Yet when do we ever hear 'holiness' preached today? I tell you, the glory and the holiness and the majesty of God must again be proclaimed in this generation. For it is not a 'lamb to the slaughter' who will soon return to this planet, but rather the risen, glorified Christ - the Judge of all the earth - before whom the apostle John says that he "fell at his feet as though dead" (Rev 1:17). It is the GLORY OF GOD that must be the deepest motivation for all true end-time ministry. Christians give all kinds of reasons for serving God - even good ones such as 'to save the lost' - but to my mind, the highest motivation by far is that of simply and utterly GLORIFYING GOD. I am convinced that this must be the primary motive for everything we do.

I truly believe that we are about to see the rise of a glorious 'street-church' in our day - gritty and anointed and real, led by men and women who like the early apostles are mostly not of 'noble birth' or of great learning, but rather have a simple and pure heart after God. These must be true men and women of prayer, of great daring and of holy power with God. And though they be ex-gang members and solo mothers, they will shake the earth by His power once again. The devil has real reason to fear such warriors as these.

I am convinced that God can only be glorified on this scale if we will allow Him to use us in accomplishing it. As the challenge that inspired evangelist D.L. Moody declared: "The world has yet to see what God will do with and for and through and in and by the man who is fully and wholly consecrated to Him." And Moody's response? - "I will try my utmost to be that man." I pray that the same may be true of each of us.

VISIT OUR WEBSITE-

www.revivalschool.com

RECOMMENDED READING:

-'The General Next to God' by Richard Collier.
-'Why Revival Tarries' by Leonard Ravenhill.
-'Revival' by Winkie Pratney. 'Azusa Street' or
-'Azusa Street' by Frank Bartleman.
-'Hollywood vs. America' by Michael Medved.
-'Life Without Father' by David Popenoe.
-'The Battle for the Mind' by Tim LaHaye.
-'What is Secular Humanism?' by Dr James Hitchcock.
-'No Compromise' by Melody Green.
-'The Closing of the American Mind' by Dr. Allan Bloom. -
'Amusing Ourselves to Death' by Neil Postman.
-'Pop goes the Gospel' by John Blanchard.

REFERENCES & QUOTATIONS

CHAPTER TWO

1. John MacArthur quote. MacArthur, J. "Ashamed of the Gospel", pg xiii - xviii.
2. Frank Bartleman quote. Bartleman, F. "Azusa Street", pg 89.
3. Samuel Chadwick quote. Source: Ravenhill, L. "Why Revival Tarries", pg 26.
4. Source: Swaggart, J. "The Pentecostal Way" as quoted in 'The Evangelist', Dec 1986, pg 6.

CHAPTER THREE

1. John Allen quote. Source: Blanchard, J. "Pop goes the Gospel", pg 98.

CHAPTER FOUR

1. Tom Morton quote. Source: Blanchard, J. "Pop goes the Gospel", pg 97.
2. Keith Green quote. Source: Green, K. "Music or Missions", as quoted Ibid. pg 141.
3. Keith Green quote. Source: Green, M. "No Compromise", pg 270.
4. Stacey Saveall quote. Src: Prophetic Email Discussion List, 3 July 1997.
5. Steve Camp quotations. Source: Styll, J.W. "Camp's 'Call' Misses the Mark, but Hits Everyone", CCM Update, 17 Nov 1997.
6. Randy Campbell news release. Source: Internet - http://jesusnorthwest.com/1998.htm
7. Lindy Warren article: "Jesus Northwest Festival Ceases Operations", CCM Update, 17 Nov 1997.

8. Gene Edward Veith article: "Whatever happened to Christian Publishing?" - 'World' Christian news magazine, Vol 12, No. 12, July 12 & July 19 1997.

CHAPTER FIVE

1. John MacArthur quote. MacArthur, J. "Ashamed of the Gospel", pg xvii- xviii.
2. John MacArthur quote. Ibid. pg xviii.

CHAPTER SIX

1. Richard Peace quote. Tapia, A. "Reaching the First Post-Christian Generation", Christianity Today, 12 Sep 1994.
2. Andres Tapia quote. Ibid.
3. Source: Humanist Manifesto's I and II, pg 16-19.

CHAPTER EIGHT

1. Early Salvation Army statistics. Bradwell, C. R. "Fight the Good Fight", pg's x, 39.
2. Ibid. pg 42.
3. Court Judge. Ibid. pg 45.
4. Ryle, J. "The Sons of Thunder." Source: Construction Site newsletter. April, 1997. Published by Storm-Harvest Ministries, Australia.

CHAPTER TEN

1. D.L. Moody's challenge. Source: K.J. Hardman, "The Spiritual Awakeners", pg 200.

Printed in the United States
210102BV00002B/560/P